P9-AOY-980

THE JEWISH

ANITA DIAMANT

SUMMIT BOOKS

ALSO BY ANITA DIAMANT

The New Jewish Wedding

BABY BOOK

NEW YORK • LONDON • TORONTO • SYDNEY • TOKYO

SUMMIT BOOKS
Simon & Schuster Building
Rockefeller Center
1230 Avenue of the Americas
New York, New York 10020

Published by SUMMIT BOOKS
SUMMIT BOOKS and colophon are trademarks
of Simon & Schuster Inc.
Designed by Edith Fowler
Manufactured in the United States of America

10 9 8 7 6 5 4 3 2

Library of Congress Cataloging-in-Publication Data

Diamant, Anita.
The Jewish baby book/Anita Diamant.
p. cm.
1. Jewish children—Religious life. 2. Baby book. 3. Names, Personal—Jewish. 4. Berit milah. 5. Judaism—Customs and practices. I. Title.
BM727.D53 1988 88-20152
296.4'4—dc19 CIP
ISBN 0-671-63935-8

For my parents
Hélène and Maurice Diamant

CONTENTS

I am a father. I have a daughter and I love her dearly. I would like my daughter to obey the commandments of the Torah; I would like her to revere me as her father. And so I ask myself the question over and over again: What is there about me that deserves the reverence of my daughter?

You see, unless I live a life that is worthy *of her reverence, I make it almost impossible for her to live a Jewish life. So many young people abandon Judaism because the Jewish models that they see in their parents are not worthy of reverence. And so, in many cases, it is the parents who make it impossible for the young to obey the Fifth Commandment.*

My message to parents is: Every day ask yourselves the question: "What is there about me that deserves the reverence of my child?"

—*Abraham Joshua Heschel*

ACKNOWLEDGMENTS

Writing acknowledgments is the icing on the cake. I have been lucky, blessed, to have had wonderful and generous teachers as sources, readers and critics. Rabbi Lawrence Kushner has been a godfather to this book. Moshe Waldoks, Howard Cooper, Billy Mencow, Rabbi Sandy Eisenberg Sasso, and Rabbi Daniel Shevitz all supplied me with invaluable assistance.

A great many people provided insight, information, and wonderful, creative ideas. Thanks are due Rabbi Susan Abramson, Elaine Adler, Dr. Joseph Adolph, Rabbi Al Axelrad, Fern Amper and Eli Schaap, Toni Bader, Naomi Bar-Yam, Judith Baskin, Dale Carre, of the National Tay-Sachs and Allied Diseases Foundation, Debra Cash, Betsy Cohen, Bradford DeMoranville, Ora Gladstone, Jane D. Gnojek, Dr. Victor Himber, Marga Kamm, Carol Katzman and Michael Katzman, Jonathan Kremer, Karen Kushner, Barbara LeFranc, Amy Mates, Phyllis Nissen, Rabbi Barbara Rosman Penzner, Rabbi Jeffrey Perry-Marx, Cantor Sam Pesserof, Stephanie Ritari, Joel Rosenberg, Arthur Samuelson, Rabbi Dennis Sasso, Cantor Robert Scherr, Alvin Schultzberg, Danny Siegel, Rabbi Daniel Siegel and Hanna Tiferet Siegel, Rabbi Rifat Soncino, Ella Taylor, Betsy Platkin Teutsch, Rabbi Edward S. Treister and Rochelle Treister, and Shoshana Zonderman and Saul E. Perlmutter.

The Jewish Women's Resource Center of the National Council of Jewish Women, New York Section, was a great source of information about ceremonies that welcome the birth of a baby girl.

This book is very much a reflection of all the people who took the time to write to me, sending copies of the ceremonies they devised for their own sons and daughters. Their ideas and energy are the reason the book exists. Special thanks are due the artists and poets whose words and images grace these pages.

My thanks also to my agent and friend, Larry Moulter. And to Jim Silberman and Dominick Anfuso at Summit Books for their enthusiastic support of *The Jewish Baby Book.*

To my friends and colleagues who withstood both gales of complaining and weeks of neglect, thank you all, especially Judy Paley, Margaret Pantridge and Sondra Stein.

My husband, Jim Ball, provided all manner of support throughout the research and writing of *The Jewish Baby Book.* In my bleakest, squeakiest hours of kvetching, he reassured and cheered me on. And during the last months of writing, when I needed uninterrupted hours, he graciously provided them.

Finally, I would never have written this book were it not for the delightful spirit who is my daughter. If I were not Emilia's mother I would not have undertaken this project, but not only because her birth showed me a gap on the bookshelf where there needed to be a book like this. Had she been a different kind of baby—a less even-tempered, predictable, happy person—I doubt that I could have mustered the concentration or energy it took to produce this volume.

PREFACE

Like so many of my middle-class American baby-boom peers, I had postponed childbearing until I was just about as grown-up and in control of my life as I was likely to get. Thirty-four years old and pregnant for the first time, I was excited, afraid, and ambivalent. I was riveted at the sight of small babies swaddled in Snugglis, strapped to their mothers and fathers. How wonderful, I thought. My husband and I were going to join this ancient sorority and fraternity of parents. On the other hand, I worried. About everything.

I asked my friends who already had children hundreds of questions—about car seats, about diaper services, about breast-feeding, about labor pains, about changes in relationships with spouses, about coping with sleeplessness, about patience. I read the books my friends had found useful. And even more important, I watched them cope and their children thrive.

Although the ultrasound suggested that the baby was a girl, my husband and I had a boy's as well as a girl's name ready. The baby would be Emilia or Eliot, in memory of my maternal grandmother, Esther Leah.

Apart from that, my husband and I did not think about the Jewish rites of passage that we might need or want once she or he arrived. Nor did we have any inkling of the overpowering, inarticulate awe we felt at the miracle of her birth—feelings that required the blessings of our tradition and our community.

After we became the proud and exhausted parents of Emilia, we scrambled to put together some sort of welcoming ritual that would coincide with my parents' visit from out of town. But it is not easy to write a ceremony that expresses the inexpressible. So there we were, searching for the right words to connect our daughter and our new family to the tradition of the people of Israel, and we found ourselves alone and lost.

The sources at our disposal were few and scattered. On the night before Emilia's *brit habat,* we found ourselves anxiously reading, writing, and typing. The ceremony was held after Shabbat morning services at Congregation Beth El of the Sudbury River Valley. It was beautiful and moving and apparently no one knew how breathless we were about the whole thing.

Some friends of ours who had boys at about the same time as we had Emilia expressed even more bewilderment. While most did not hesitate to have their sons circumcised, their lack of understanding about the religious significance of the rite, and about how they might participate in it, left them feeling dazed, out of control, and something less than joyful at their sons' *brisses.*

I wrote *The Jewish Baby Book* to be a resource for new parents, their families and communities as they commemorate the joy of their new babies in ways that both reflect the traditions and wisdom of our ancestors, and look forward to the promise of the new life among us.

The *Midrash* says, "With each child, the world begins anew."

Dear Reader, if you are looking at these words while preparing for the arrival of a child, I wish you an easy wait, a short labor, and a healthy baby—who sleeps.

Anita Diamant
Newton, Massachusetts
January 1988
Tevet 5748

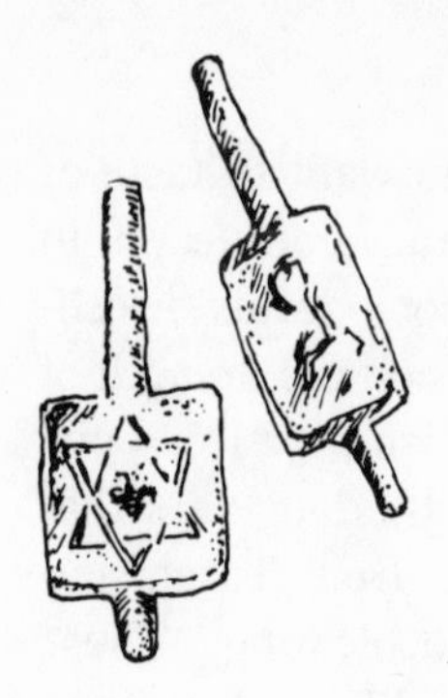

INTRODUCTION

"Be fruitful and multiply" is the first *mitzvah*—the first commandment—in the Bible. For Jews, having children is both a primary religious obligation and the crown of human life—a fundamental duty and the source of the greatest human happiness. Thus, the arrival of a new baby has always been greeted with joyful ceremonies and customs. *The Jewish Baby Book* is part of that long and varied tradition.

This book is different from all the other baby books on your nightstand. It has nothing to say about Kegel exercises or breathing through labor pains. In these pages you will find no advice about nursing, cradle cap, or sibling rivalry. *The Jewish Baby Book* is about the first Jewish decisions you will be called upon to make as parents—decisions about names and about ways to welcome your child into the convenant of the Jewish people.

The Jewish Baby Book describes the wide range of liberal* Jewish practice in America. In this evolving marriage of old and new, customs with a four-thousand-year-old history are being rediscovered and celebrated in modern idioms. Now, before the ice cream and cake are served at Rebecca's gala first birthday party, the guests sing *shehehiyanu,* the traditional prayer of thanksgiving for beginnings, and recall the celebration of Isaac's weaning in the book of Genesis.

* *Liberal Judaism refers to all non-Orthodox movements.*

This book provides a menu for people who want to taste of Judaism's mythic, historic, religious and literary cornucopia to discover what Jewish tradition offers to you now, at this threshold in your lives. *The Jewish Baby Book* draws on the breadth of Jewish experience, from the most ancient Jewish practice of circumcision to the new covenant rituals for baby daughters that reflect feminism's gift to Jewish observance; from Torah and Talmud to previously unpublished poems and blessings. These pages document how Judaism lives and gives life to Jews who call themselves Reform, Conservative, Reconstructionist or traditional/egalitarian.

Our great-grandparents would have been mystified by a book like this. In the close-knit Jewish communities of the past, most people participated in the rituals associated with birth long before they became parents so they knew what to do. For most American Jews, however, "community" is more a wistful goal than a weekly gathering. Many of us find ourselves rediscovering and reconstructing Jewish practice as we move from one milestone, one rite of passage, to the next.

New parents who want to make meaningful decisions about Jewish names and celebrations for their babies often find themselves at sea. Most people affiliate with the Jewish community by joining a synagogue when their children reach school age, so many parents-to-be and new moms and dads lack comfortable access to the Jewish "experts"—rabbis, cantors, *mohels*—who could help provide resources and guide choices.

Besides, few expectant parents worry about Jewish rites of passage until after the baby is born. You've got plenty to think about as it is! If this is your first child, you are devouring pregnancy and childbirth books in preparation for the Big Day. If you have other children, you've probably marshaled all your strength to get through this pregnancy without selling one of the older ones.

Another reason that Jewish parents avoid preparing for the ritual welcoming of a new baby is the evil eye. Really! Even in America in the twentieth century, it is common to find Jewish parents-to-be reluctant to bring a crib into the house until the baby is born, out of inarticulate superstitions rooted in Eastern European folklore.

So what happens is that you find yourselves wanting to have a meaningful, thoughtful rite of passage for your wonderful new baby at precisely the time you have the least energy to prepare for one. *The Jewish Baby Book* is the resource for this special time.

The first section, "*Chai*—Life," is about the mystery and awe of pregnancy and birth. From private moments alone with your spouse to newly imagined baby showers, this chapter helps you acknowledge and celebrate powerful emotions in distinctively Jewish ways.

As parents, your baby's name is the first Jewish decision you make and "A Jewish Name" provides a historical context for that all-important choice of what to call your baby. The lists of names for boys and girls are full of suggestions from around the world, some as old as the Bible, some newer than the land of Israel.

The next portion of *The Jewish Baby Book* is entitled *Brit,* which means covenant. The Jews are often described as the choosing people—a people who choose to enter into a covenant with God, a relationship that involves mutual obligations. From the beginning of Jewish history that relationship has been sealed by *bris* or *brit milah,* the covenant of circumcision. At this point in Jewish history there are new covenant ceremonies for our daughters called by many names, including *brit habat,* the covenant of the daughter. Different as they are, both *bris* and *brit habat* initiate our children into the covenant and into the people of Israel.

The covenant section is divided into three parts, the first of which concerns *bris* and includes everything parents need to know about its laws, rituals and customs. Here you will also find a guide to the historical, biblical, and theological underpinnings of *brit milah;* a discussion of the complex post-Freudian response to circumcision; advice on how to find and talk to a *mohel;* and information about special cases like circumcision for adoption.

The chapter on *brit habat* is a guide to a rite-of-passage in the making. Ceremonies that celebrate the birth of a daughter draw on traditional Sephardic practice, as well as new-minted prayers and practices. This section contains a number of sample ceremonies as well as a menu of the prayers and ritual elements most commonly included in *brit habat* ceremonies.

The third part of the section on covenants is called *"Hiddur Mitzvah:* Beautiful Touches," and includes suggestions for ways to enhance the celebration of *brit milah* or *brit habat* with ritual objects, music, and words.

Whatever your circumstances—whether you know the sex of your unborn child, if your baby is already here, or if you are adopting—I encourage you to read through the entire *brit* section. Not only will it provide you with a historical context for your family's celebration, but you just might find an idea, reading or translation that would be perfect for your child's *brit* ceremony in a section you might think is irrelevant.

Part Four of this book, *"Simcha:* Joy" is meant to help you celebrate. The chapter on announcements talks about spreading news in distinctively Jewish ways, with suggestions and examples. Since Jewish law commands that there be a *seudat mitzvah* —a meal—after a *brit,* "Simcha Means Party" contains information about food, photography, gifts, and ways of making your celebration a delight for all concerned. "Celebrations and Customs" describes the full round of parties and practices that surround the arrival of a baby, from the very ancient *pidyon haben* or redemption of the firstborn, to the "twinning" of *brit* ceremonies, linking American Jews to families in the Soviet Union who are not free to observe or celebrate.

The section entitled "Modern Life" raises a Jewish perspective on medical technologies employed to help infertile couples conceive, as well as mechanisms for testing the health of the unborn. The chapter on adoption acknowledges this as an increasingly common way that Jews are fulfilling the commandment to "be fruitful and multiply." This section covers everything from Jewish law regarding adoption to resources for Jewish adoptive families and to adoption ceremonies.

Finally, "The First Year" describes some of the ways that parents are celebrating the seasons of the first special year with a new baby, from the first Shabbat at home together to parties that celebrate a child's weaning.

Nothing unites people so joyfully as the birth of a baby. However, even on this happiest of occasions, the Jewish community finds itself embroiled in contentious debates. Although Judaism has never been monolithic in practice or belief, pluralism has probably never been as public or as rancorous a fact of Jewish life as it is today. The ancient question Who is a Jew? reverberates loudly in America, where the Jewish community, already divided into denominations, includes increasing numbers of Jews by choice and Jews by adoption, as well as interfaith couples and their children.

Who is a Jew? Modern realities have added a few new twists to the ancient question. In a radical departure from tradition and from the practice of Conservative and Orthodox Jews, the Reform and Reconstructionist movements recognize as Jews all children of one Jewish parent—father or mother—if those children are given a Jewish education and affirm a Jewish identity. Many Orthodox rabbis in the United States and Israel contest the Jewishness of those whose conversions were supervised by non-Orthodox rabbis.

Who is a Jew? The question has been answered in the language of *halachah,* psychology, sociology, and anthropology. It is taken up in novels, sermons, responsa, and movement platforms. It is a question that binds Jews to each other, even as it tears them apart.

The poet Muriel Rukeyser wrote, "To be a Jew in the twentieth century is to be offered a gift." For the purposes of *The Jewish Baby Book,* a Jew is someone who accepts the gift, opens it and wrestles with its maddening, life-giving contradictions—and then passes the gift along so that it can be given again.

Every Jewish baby is a link in a chain that extends back to Sinai, when according to *Midrash,* the souls of all the Jews—even those yet unborn—were present for the giving of the Torah.

Every Jewish baby is a triumph of life over death, especially in a century that has witnessed the annihilation of so many Jewish children.

And every Jewish baby embodies the ancient longing for redemption, for a world as innocent and peaceful as a newborn's face.

The story is told: God commands us to perform countless acts of love. But how can we begin to obey such a difficult commandment? The answer lies (or soon will lie) in your arms. Every smile, every diaper change, every sleepless night, every lullaby, every wordless prayer of thanks for this baby—in these and the unending ways we care for and teach and protect our children, we perform countless acts of love. And the world is made holier. And so are we.

PART ONE

CHAI: LIFE

CONCEPTION

Judaism, which sanctifies so many of life's passages with *brachot* and *mitzvot*—prayers and sacred obligations—is comparatively silent about conception, pregnancy and birth, the most awesome of all human transitions. Until recently, and within the Orthodox community still, the expectation of conception began with marriage. The bridal *mikvah,* ritual immersion before marriage, not only marked the beginning of a woman's sexual activity, but her decision to become a mother as well as a wife.[1]

Mikvah, however, is foreign to most American Jews. And marriage typically precedes childbearing by years. Still, the decision to begin or add a new child to a family is so important that some people have created simple, private rituals to mark their decision in distinctly Jewish ways.

Deciding to have a child alters a couple's sexual relationship. Physical pleasure now becomes a means to what Judaism considers a sacred end. And so momentous a choice seems to call for a self-conscious *havdalah,* or separation, between one stage of life and another.

Jewish tradition encourages lovemaking on Shabbat, on Friday night in particular. According to the *Midrash,* the Sabbath reunites God's male and female aspects. And the joy, peace and relaxation associated with Friday evening, was thought to be a particularly auspicious time for conception.[2]

In terms of the rhythms of modern life, Friday night also happens to be a perfect time to make a separation between one way of doing things and another. The work week is over. It is time to concentrate on each other.

There are no rules. There is barely any precedent for these private moments. You choose what you feel comfortable with: a special and leisurely meal, lit by Shabbat candles. Perhaps a bubble bath. Reading the *ketubah* hung over the bed or simply reciting the *shehehiyanu*—the prayer of thanks that marks all manner of beginnings. The blessing and drinking of wine from the cups used at your wedding, or singing the *sheva b'rachot,* the seven wedding blessings. And love.

When the Baal Shem Tov, the great Jewish mystic, was asked why people love children so much, he answered that a child is still very close to his or her conception. And since there was so much ecstasy at the conception, it still shows in the child.

Some choose to acknowledge their decision to become Jewish parents with *mikvah.* The uses of the ritual bath are not limited to menstruating women. *Mikvah* is a way of preparing for various kinds of encounters with the Holy, with the source of life and death. Some traditional Jews—men and women—visit the *mikvah* before every Shabbat, as well as in preparation for Yom Kippur. According to Jewish folklore, *mikvah* is an antidote for infertility.

The traditional blessing for *mikvah* is:

בָּרוּךְ אַתָּה יְיָ, אֱלֹהֵינוּ מֶלֶךְ הָעוֹלָם אֲשֶׁר קִדְּשָׁנוּ בְּמִצְוֹתָיו, וְצִוָּנוּ עַל הַטְבִילָה.

Baruch ata Adonai Eloheynu Melech Ha-olam asher kid'shanu be-mitzvotav vitsivanu al ha'tevilah.

Praised are you, Adonai, God of all Creation, who sanctifies us with your commandments and commands us concerning immersion.

A *kavannah,* or intentional prayer, on such an occasion might be:

Now as I immerse myself, I begin a new cycle, a cycle of rebirth and renewal in Your world and Your people Israel. I prepare in hopes of creating new life according to the *mitzvah* of *pe'ru ur'vu,** and for the sanctification of that life in *huppah, Torah v' maasim tovim.*†[3]

* *Be fruitful and multiply, the first* mitzvah.
† Huppah, *the marriage canopy; Torah, Jewish learning;* maasim tovim, *acts of loving-kindness.*

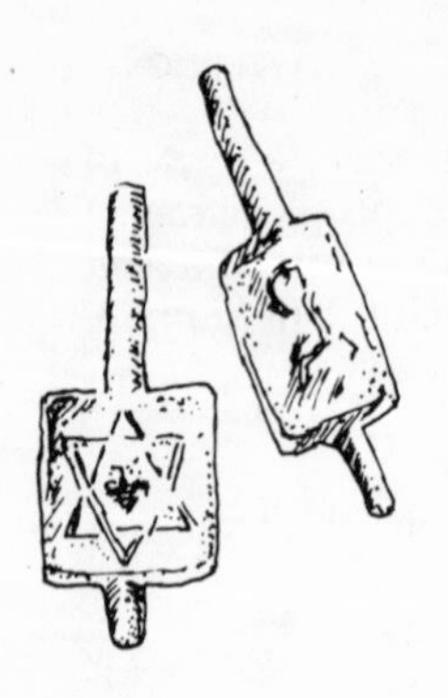

PREGNANCY

Pregnant women have always evoked respect, affection, and excitement in the Jewish community. In *shtetl* life, pregnant women were pampered and protected because it was believed that any unpleasantness might adversely affect the outcome. And in many communities pains were taken not to let the evil spirits know that a baby was due. In particular the demon known as Lilith, Adam's first wife, was thought to attack newborns.[4]

Shabbat can provide couples with a way of privately marking the milestones of pregnancy. After the bustle of the week (and after the older children are asleep), Friday night can be the perfect time to recall the "events" of the week: the end of morning sickness, the first kick, the first meeting of the childbirth class.

Whether or not you think of yourselves as religious people, pregnancy makes everyone a supplicant. Mostly, the prayers of expectant parents are simple: Dear God, please make it a healthy baby. (Also, please make these hemorrhoids go away.) While such fervent requests of God will not be found in the synagogue prayer book, prayers like these are as old as memory and were published as *tehinnot,* the Yiddish petitionary prayers of Eastern European women. Our great-grandmothers doubtless shared many prayers for their baby's health and for an easy birth, but that tradition is largely lost to us.

There is a formal set of prayers said during pregnancy by traditional Jews, one prescribed for the mother, and three to be recited by the father-to-be during the daily prayer service during the third, seventh, and ninth months of pregnancy—one in each trimester.[5] Many Jews are uncomfortable with the language of these prayers, and with the fact that most are the sole responsibility of the father.

Pregnancy has inspired Jewish parents to write new prayers and poems that express the anticipation and excitement of this special time. This prayer, written during her pregnancy by Rabbi Judy Shanks, revives the tradition of *tehinnot* in modern terms.

With all my heart, with all my soul, with all my might,
I pray for the health of this child.
I pray for it to be perfect in mind and body,
To issue safely and easily from me
At the proper time,
To grow steadily and sturdily
In a home filled with joy at its presence,
To be nurtured into a person who greets the world with passion, enthusiasm, dance, love, humility, faith.

With all my heart, with all my soul, with all my might,
I pray for the health of this world.
I beg its leaders to temper their insanity with reason,
So that my child may be born into a world that seeks longevity, not annihilation.
Let the world join in the thrill of creation,
And turn its back on the lust for destruction.
Let my child never know the pain and absurdity of warfare
Let it take part in the dances of peace.

With all my heart, with all my soul, with all my might,
I pray for God to watch over me and my family,
I pray for strength and courage when I labor to bring forth this child,
I pray for the capacity to return my husband's love for me,
I pray for the ability to love and nurture this child,
I pray to feel God's presence now and always.[6]

Celebrating Pregnancy

Although pregnancy and childbirth have become much more of a joint adventure for expectant fathers and mothers, the physical changes and challenges of having a baby makes sisters of all mothers. Jewish women have taken advantage of two old customs to celebrate this special time in life: *rosh hodesh,* and the good old American baby shower.

Rosh hodesh, the celebration of the new moon, is a semiholiday that falls on the first day of every lunar month. In traditional observance of *rosh hodesh* women were exempt from all work. For the past twenty years some American and Israeli women have formed groups that meet to celebrate *rosh hodesh* (literally, the "head of the month") with study, prayer, liturgy, and rituals that celebrate the unique qualities of Jewish women's spirituality. *Rosh hodesh* groups have created beautiful ceremonies of preparation for their pregnant members, and also rituals of passage for women who are newly delivered.[7]

Two examples of creative pregnancy celebrations follow.

Marci's Baby Shower

Marci's best friend and sister-in-law decided to host a very special baby shower for her. All the guests who were mothers—including Marci's own mom—were asked to contribute photographs of themselves pregnant and photographs of their babies. These were collected into a large album, with a picture of the very pregnant Marci on the cover, and space for the new baby's photos.

Among the gifts of teddy bears and stretch suits were gift certificates for home-cooked Shabbat meals, Jewish children's books, and a blue and white *tsedakah* (charity) box for the baby's room. One friend made a tape of soothing, distracting music for Marci to use during labor. And Marci's mother-in-law bought a beautiful *mezuzah* to hang on the nursery door.

Before everyone left, Marci's cousin, who happens to be a

rabbi, concluded the festivities with a prayer none of the guests had ever heard before:

מוֹדֶה אֲנוּ לְפָנֵי הַשְּׁכִינָה, מֵעֵין חַיֵּי עוֹלָם, שֶׁנִּבְרֵאתִי אִשָּׁה וְנוֹצְרוּ בִּי כּוֹחוֹת הַחַיִּים.

Modah ani lifnay ha-Sh'china, may-ayn cha-yay olam, she'nivrayti isha v'notzru bi kochot ha-chayim.

I am thankful before the Shechinah, the source of the life of the world, who created me a woman and created in me the powers of life.

בְּרוּכָה אַתְּ יְיָ אֱלֹהֵינוּ וֵאלוֹהֵי אִמּוֹתֵינוּ וַאֲבוֹתֵינוּ אֲשֶׁר סִדְּרָה אֶת הַלְּבָנָה בְּדַרְכָּהּ וְסִדְּרָה אֶת מַחְזוֹרֵי הַחַיִּים. בְּרוּכָה אַתְּ יְיָ שֶׁעֲשָׂתַנִי אִשָּׁה.

B'rucha at Adonai Eloheynu vaylohay imotaynu v'avotaynu asher sidrah et ha-l'vana b'darkah v'sidrah et machzoray ha-chayim.
B'rucha at Adonai, she'astani isha.

Blessed are you Adonai our God and God of our foremothers and forefathers, who has set the moon in its path and has set the order of the cycles of life. Blessed are you, Adonai, who has created me a woman.[8]

Shoshana's Pre-Birth Ceremony

Eleven women were invited to join Shoshana's long-standing *rosh hodesh* group. Each guest was asked to bring a fruit that symbolized a wish for the mother-to-be, and an egg-shaped candle, the egg being an ancient and universal symbol of fertility. As Shoshana lit a pair of candles, she recited her Hebrew name and her matrilineage: Shoshana bat* Rivka, bat Sarah, bat Esther Malka. The flame was passed to the woman next to her, who in

* Bat—*daughter of.*

turn gave her name and the names of her mother, grandmother, and great-grandmother. This was followed by the *shehehiyanu.*

Next came a breathing/relaxation exercise, and then blessings over and sharing a crescent-shaped challah and sweet wine. Then, each woman gave Shoshana a gift of fruit and a wish: an apple with wishes for wisdom; a pineapple for patience; and figs for strength.

Songs and *niggunim,* wordless prayerlike melodies, were sung. The ceremony concluded with a blessing over eating of the fruits arrayed before them, which made a nice transition into an evening filled with more food, conversation, and laughter.[9]

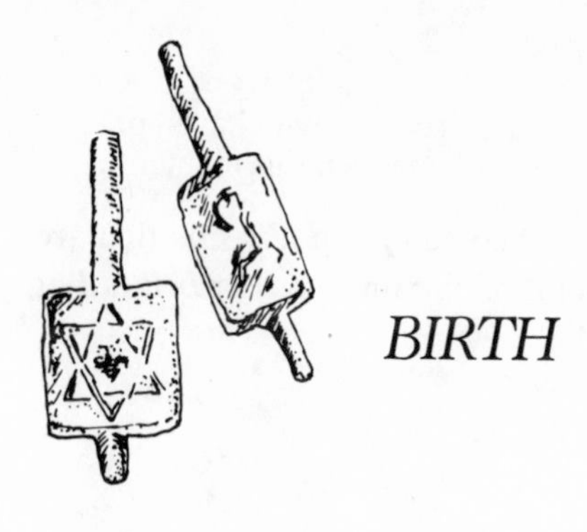

BIRTH

Agony, joy, wonder, terror, laughter, anger, tears, remembering to breathe, crying out, despair, courage, awe. The struggle, pain, and hope of giving birth is the most intense encounter with the Holy that most of us will ever know.

When the baby is born—held, kissed, studied, cradled, nursed, admired—language seems utterly inadequate. At this special moment, when there are no words, the tradition provides two simple prayers.[10]

בָּרוּךְ אַתָּה יְיָ, אֱלֹהֵינוּ מֶלֶךְ הָעוֹלָם הַטּוֹב וְהַמֵּטִיב.

Baruch ata Adonai, Eloheynu Melech Ha-olam Ha-tov ve-hamativ.

Blessed are You, Adonai, Ruler of Creation, Who is good and does good.

and

בָּרוּךְ אַתָּה יְיָ, אֱלֹהֵינוּ מֶלֶךְ הָעוֹלָם שֶׁהֶחֱיָנוּ וְקִיְּמָנוּ וְהִגִּיעָנוּ לַזְּמַן הַזֶּה:

Baruch ata Adonai, Eloheynu Melech Ha-olam shehehiyanu vikiamanu vihigiani lazman hazeh.

Blessed are You, Adonai, Ruler of Creation, who has kept us alive, and sustained us and enabled us to reach this moment.

The other traditional words that come to mind, words that are repeated at a *brit milah* (covenant of circumcision) or *brit habat* (covenant of the daughter) are:

בָּרוּךְ הַבָּא

Baruch haba.

Blessed is he who comes.

בְּרוּכָה הַבָּאָה.

Bracha haba'a.

Blessed is she who comes.

PART TWO

NAMING YOUR JEWISH BABY

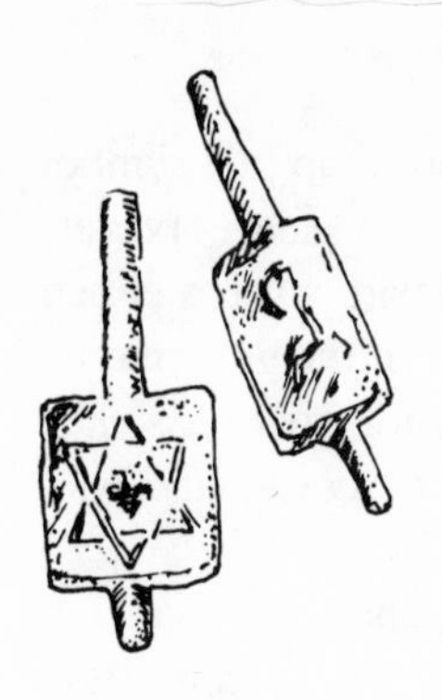

WHAT'S IN A NAME?

Few parents approach the subject of their child's name with indifference. Some people have names selected before they conceive; some spend the nine months of pregnancy poring over lists and ask friends and relatives for feedback on their top contenders; others wait until after the baby is born before settling on what to call him or her. Some couples keep the name they select for their child a secret and others refer to the mother's belly by its soon-to-be name.

For Jews a name is a complicated gift, one that bestows identity and generational connection. It can also reflect religious and spiritual dimensions, while giving a voice to parental aspirations. Choosing your baby's name is a second conception. It is an exercise of power and creativity, like Adam's in the garden. Names are often living testaments to people who have died, and a link to all the Daniels and Rebeccas back to the beginning of our people. Naming is also an act of faith and hope that your children will not only remember their namesakes, but act as they have, to create a better future. Naming begins the process of shaping the person—hopefully the *mensch*—your child will become.

What's in a Name? Names are powerful magic. *HaShem,* The Name, is one of the most common ways of referring to God. Not only is God's real name unpronounceable, The Name is unknowable because there is a sense in which it is more than just symbol or signifier. The Name mysteriously contains the essence, power, and unity that is God. The great founder of Hasidism, Israel ben Eliezer, was called the Baal Shem Tov, master of the good name, not simply because he enjoyed a reputation for goodness. His name suggested that the man knew more of the power and wisdom of The Name than most people.

The Bible portrays naming as the first independent human act. Adam's job in Eden was to name the beasts of the field and the birds of the air and every living thing. This was no make-work project. The Hebrew for "word," *davar,* is also the Hebrew for "thing." Thus, the names and essences of temporal things are also seen as being the same in some fundamental way. There is something about human names that somehow confirms this insight. A woman named Rose, by any other name, would somehow be someone other than Rose. Rose is Rose, just as Esther is, unalterably, Esther.

The Torah underscores the importance of names in its attention to dramatic name changes. Abram and Sarai become different people—Abraham and Sarah—once they accept the covenant and become the parents of the Jewish people. Even more dramatic is the name change of Jacob, "supplanter," who after struggling with the angel, is given the name Israel, "wrestler with God," and becomes the patriarch of the twelve tribes.

Proverb 22 says, "A good name is rather to be chosen than good oil," oil being a measure of wealth. "A good name" probably refers to reputation, but the sense that names contain an inherent value and power is strong in the tradition. There is a story that the Jews enslaved in Egypt had become otherwise lax in their faith under their oppression. Even so, they were saved from total assimilation by keeping two identifying signs that set them apart: They retained the custom of circumcision and they held on to their Hebrew names.

Acknowledging the importance of naming, the *Midrash* advises, "One should examine names carefully in order to give his son a name that is worthy so that the son may become a righteous person, for sometimes the name is a contributing factor for good as for evil." Still, the power attributed to "good" names is only as strong as the people who bear them. The tradition stresses that a good name is really earned. The *Mishnah* says, "The crown of a good name excels all other crowns, including the crown of learning, of priesthood and even of royalty."[1]

NAMES IN THE BIBLE

During biblical times, people had only one name and every child was given a freshly minted name that was entirely his or her own. Over a thousand years, there is only one Abraham, one Sarah, one Miriam, one Solomon. None of the twenty-one kings of Judah was named after David, the founder of the dynasty.

There are 2,800 personal names in the Bible, of which less than 5 percent are used today.[2] Biblical names are a wonderfully mixed bag. Many are theophoric—exalting God. Names with the prefixes or suffixes *el, eli, ya, yahu* all refer to the Holy One: Elisha—God is my salvation; Raphael—God has healed; Netanyahu—gift of God; Michael—who is like God.

Some biblical names describe the particular circumstances of a child's birth. Moses means "because I drew him out of the water." Chava (the Hebrew name of Eve) comes from the root word for life, "because she was the mother of all living generations."

Nature names abound in the Bible, resembling nothing so much as those of American Indians: Deborah—bee; Jonah—dove; Tamar—palm tree. This tradition has been revived with a passion in modern Israel; Tal and Tali—dew; Elon and Elana—oak; Oren—fir tree; Namir—leopard.

SACRED AND SECULAR

Despite their importance and durability, biblical Hebrew names have always competed with names from other languages and cultures. Even during the Talmudic period, Aramaic, Greek and Roman names outnumbered biblical names among Jews. During the Middle Ages in Eastern Europe, Jewish males were usually given both a secular (*kinnui*) and a religious name (*shem ha-kadosh*). Eventually, the secular name became so dominant that some parents did not bother with the Hebrew one, a development that alarmed the rabbis so much that they decreed every boy had to be given a Hebrew name, a ruling that is still in effect.[3]

Still, it remained common for men to have two names, one for use in the gentile world, the other for religious purposes. The process for selecting secular names varied. The most straightforward method was to seek a direct translation of a Hebrew name; thus in France, men called Chaim in synagogue were often known as Vive on the street. In Germany, the use of the first name Wolf was probably based on the biblical Benjamin, whose tribe was associated with that animal. However, it was just as common to select a secular name because it sounded like a Hebrew name, or shared a letter or two with a Hebrew name, or simply because it was popular in the surrounding culture.

Girls rarely had two names. The one that sufficed was often, though by no means always, Hebrew. Through constant use, Yiddish and Ladino names took on the venerable status of biblical ones. Feigel, for example, a very popular name among our Polish great-grandparents, has an obscure etymology and may be based on words meaning violet, bird, or even fig.[4] These Yiddish names often pose a problem for modern parents who go looking for Grandma's Hebrew name.

Customs differed in the Sephardic world. Although girls were commonly given only a non-Hebrew name, boys in Syria, for example, would never be called by an Arabic name only. Equivalents in Hebrew and Arabic would be hyphenated, as in Shelomo-Shelem (peace) or Yehuda-Aslan (lion).[5]

Hebrew names remained essential to men's prayer life—for being called to the Torah, and for use on legal documents such as *ketubot* (marriage contracts). Since it was thought that the angels speak only Hebrew, one needed to know his Hebrew name in order to gain access to heaven. Additionally, it was essential to know the Hebrew names of both one's parents; in the memorial service, the name of the departed and his father are invoked, and in the special prayer recited on behalf of the sick, the name of the patient's mother is included.

With emancipation in Europe, names were more readily taken from society at large, softening the lines between Jew and gentile.* But by end of the nineteenth century in Northern Europe and in early twentieth century America there developed a whole new category of Jewish-gentile names. Jews seemed drawn to certain names; in pre-World War I Germany, for example, Ludwig, Moritz and Siegfried were so identified with Jews, that non-Jews began to avoid them. Isadore (which actually means "gift of Isis") was a very popular *kinnui* for Isaac and Israel, and became so identified with the Jews that it became a Nazi epithet.[6] In America, Hymie, a nickname for Hyman, which was a popular "Americanization" of Chaim, became an anti-Semitic slur as well.

Jewish immigrants to America often selected new names when they arrived in the *goldene medina,* the golden land. Although some traditional names (Abraham and Sarah, for example) never completely disappeared, many Yiddish and Hebrew names seemed too foreign, too "green" for the new country. So the Yiddish Blume (flower) blossomed into Rose, Lily, and Iris. The old country Tsvi (deer) who was known in Yiddish as Hersch (deer) became Harry.

The American custom has been to give children both a secular name and a Hebrew name. Often, the two share nothing but the initial sound. A baby girl named for her grandmother Shayna

* *The history of Jewish surnames is a fascinating story unto itself. It was not until the Middle Ages in Europe that Jews commonly added family names, mostly to facilitate dealings with the non-Jewish world. In Northern Europe, Jews did not take family names until the nineteenth century, and then often under compulsion by Christian authorities.*

thus becomes Sandra or Susan. A boy named for Uncle Moshe may be called to the Torah as Moshe, but his friends will call him Mark. Actually "phonetic assimilation" has ancient precedents; under Greek rule, Menachem often became Menelaus.

NAMING AFTER RELATIVES

Naming children after parents or grandparents is not found in the Bible, but the custom dates back to Egyptian Jews of the sixth century B.C.E., who most likely borrowed the idea from their neighbors. The custom of naming a child after a relative to perpetuate his or her memory has been common ever since.

It is a constant source of amazement to Jews of Ashkenazic descent, who name children after relatives who have passed away, that Sephardim name children after living relatives. In some Sephardic communities, the practice follows a precise pattern: the first son is named after the father's father, the first daughter is named after the father's mother; the second son is named after the mother's father, the second daughter after the mother's mother. Beyond that, names may be selected to honor any family member or friend.[7]

In America it is common to give a baby the same Hebrew name as the person honored, and then select a secular name on the basis of the initial letter or sound of the Hebrew, which explains how it came to pass that Baruch ("blessed") becomes Barry, Bradley, Bruce and even Brian, a Celtic or Gaelic name that means strength. And one Grandma Naomi of blessed memory was honored with a namesake called Natalie, which means Christmas child.

SUPERSTITION

Names have been associated with witchcraft since the beginning of human speech, probably due to the global suspicion that the soul is identical with and identified by a person's name. Thus, in some cultures, a secret name—one that expresses a person's true self—is given at birth and guarded against enemies and evil forces.

Superstitions about the power of names abound in Jewish culture and are even acknowledged in the Talmud, which states, "Four things can abrogate the fate of man and they are: charity, supplication, change of name and change of action." Thus, when the angel of death came looking for someone, a shrewd person would say, "I am not the one you are seeking. I am not the one who committed the sins you charge me with."

Name changes were often employed to fool the angel of death. Given the high infant mortality rate of earlier times, it is easy to understand why the angel of death and demons were thought to be particularly drawn to babies. In Poland, newborns who were ill or somehow at risk were given names like Alte, Alter (another, or old one) or Zaida (grampa) to confuse evil spirits like Lilith, who reputedly searched the earth for Jewish infants. Not only would such a name confuse death, who would come looking for a baby but find an old man instead, it also implied that the child would fulfill the name and live many years. Similarly, a name like Chaim (life) was given as a talisman.

For this reason, the Ashkenazim shunned the practice of naming children after living relatives, lest the grim reaper take a child in place of a grandfather. Sephardic Jews had a different attitude toward the angel of death, assuming he might err in favor of longevity for both generations if fathers and sons bore the same name.

American Jews, who would mock such medieval fantasies, in practice tend to follow the advice of the medieval pietist Rabbi

Judah HaHasid who wrote, "Although one should not believe in superstitions, it is better to be careful." Thus, you find couples who refuse to have a crib in the house before the baby is born lest they tempt the evil eye; and parents who would no sooner consider naming their baby after a living grandparent than leave the baby outside in a snowstorm.

NAMES AND TRENDS

Throughout history, rabbis and scholars have bemoaned the demise of authentic Jewish names and warned against the assimilationism of choosing secular names for children. But the mish-mash of Jewish naming is at least as old as the destruction of the Temple.

Throughout history, names have been as vulnerable to fashion as hemlines. The Talmudic period saw a burst of new Hebrew names (Mier, Nahman, Ahavah) as well as a revival of obscure ones (Hillel and Gamliel). But even then many Jews were giving their babies distinctly non-Jewish names from the vernacular, which for many generations was Aramaic.

It would be simpleminded to view only the most ancient Hebrew names as kosher. Jewish names were not handed down from Sinai, they have been hammered out of history. Take one Jewish name: Esther. Esther is Persian in origin and shares its root with Astarte and Ishtar, the great fertility goddesses of the ancient Middle East. Although Esther is Hadassah in Hebrew, no one could argue the Jewish pedigree of Esther. Mordecai, the other hero of the Purim story, also has a Persian name, and an idolatrous one at that, since it means "devotee of the god Marduk."

Jewish use of non-Jewish names has been a constant source of irritation to those who consider themselves conservators of the tradition. The Hellenization of Jewish names (Jason for Joshua) dismayed the rabbis of late antiquity. Alexander, a name with a decidedly un-Jewish source, has enjoyed a loyal following since biblical times and continues to be extremely popular.

Every generation adopts a new set of names that reflect the changing fashion of the times. In America, the children of Rose, Molly and Sophie, of Sam, Max and Jacob were Sylvia, Rosalyn, and Muriel, Arthur, Charles, and Leonard.

They in turn named children Ellen, Gail, and Karen, Alan, Barry, and Ken, who raised the generation of Kim, Jennifer, and Stacey, Bradley, Joshua, and Jesse.

The most recent pattern of Jewish American naming is a return to roots. Biblical names like Sarah and Benjamin, Rebecca and Aaron are enormously popular. And, interestingly, there has also been a run on selected "ethnic" immigrant names that "feel" Jewish; thus the rash of announcements proclaiming a new generation of Rose and Lily and Max and Sam. Another new fashion, especially among Jews who have spent time in Israel, is to give babies modern Hebrew names.

Today, rabbis of all denominations tend to advocate the selection of an identifiably Jewish name. One of their most compelling arguments is that names like Ruth and David, Shulamit and Raphael make life simpler because such names work well in the three settings American Jews are likely to inhabit: in thoroughly American situations like public school; in religious life, as when one is called to the Torah; and as a visitor to—or resident of—Israel.

MODERN HEBREW NAMES

One of the biggest changes in the lexicon of Jewish names has occurred since the late 1800s, when Eliezer Ben-Yehuda began the movement to make Hebrew a modern language. With the establishment of the Hebrew-speaking state of Israel, a host of new Hebrew names were added to newly-popular ancient ones.

Many who came to Palestine after the Holocaust were anxious to cast off all reminders of the Diaspora, especially Germanic names. Some were translated from Yiddish to Hebrew; Shayna (meaning pretty one) became Yaffa, Gittel (meaning good one) became Tovah. Others simply chose a Hebrew name. Reversing the old custom, they picked one on the basis of a sound or letter, so Mendel and Moritz became Menachem and Meir.

The first generation of sabras born in Israel inspired a host of new names. There were translations; a baby girl named for her aunt Raizel (Rose) would be called Varda. And there was a resurrection of ancient biblical names that had not been heard for generations: Amnon, Yoram, Avital, Tamar. Even names of evil characters surfaced, such as Aviram, who was swallowed by the earth in retribution for his rebellion against Moses.

As the people gave life to the land, the land gave names to their babies: Kinneret (a sea), Arnon (a wadi), Barak (lightning), and Ora (light). Boys' names inspired a generation of girls' names: Ariella from Ariel, Gabriella from Gabriel. And there are many names that serve both boys and girls in *Eretz Yisrael,* including Yona—dove; Ayala and Ayal—deer; Leor and Leora—light; Liron and Lirona—song.

The self-consciousness among settlers that Jewish history was being made led to the creation of names like Aliyah (wave of immigration), Or-Tzion (light of Zion), and even Balfour and Balfouria (for the British Foreign Secretary who issued a declaration announcing England's favorable attitude toward the establishment of a Jewish state in Palestine).

Israeli names have a music and life of their own. A recent trend has been the addition of a final tav or "t" sound to the end of virtually all girls' names, adding an extra feminine emphasis to even the most ancient; thus Leah has become Le'at. One American who moved to Israel wrote, "It is of course the traditional names that give rise to all those icky diminutives: Yosef (Yossi), Avraham (Avi), Yaakov (Kobi), Yitzchak (Itzik and Tzachi).

David inevitably becomes . . . Dudu, which to me always evokes a disposable diaper.

"Rachel meanwhile yields Racheli and Rochi, Shoshana is truncated to Shoshi, Ruth Ruti, Channah Channi, and my own Esther becomes Esti."[8]

THE LISTS, AND HOW TO USE THEM

No list of names can be complete. The compilation that follows is not a scholarly work or a definitive dictionary, but a guide and tool for parents seeking a name for a Jewish child of the English-speaking world of the late twentieth century. Not all of the 2,800 names that appear in the Bible are listed; for instance, you will not find the long-suffering Job here. Nor can there be any comprehensive catalog of modern Hebrew names; Israeli society propagates new ones so quickly, any list is incomplete before the ink dries. The names below simply reflect the author's best effort to catalog names that conform to current tastes and trends.

While you may find all the help you need on the following pages, there are other places to turn. A sympathetic rabbi, cantor, or *mohel* can be a great help. And if you want some advice in selecting a modern Hebrew name, talk to an Israeli.*

All the names on the lists below have a Jewish pedigree of some sort, although with a little effort you can find a Jewish precedent for the use of almost any name, including Christian.

* *The best published resource is* The Complete Dictionary of English and Hebrew Names *by Alfred J. Kolatch (Jonathan David Publishers, 1984). A volume of nearly five hundred pages, Kolatch's book includes a remarkable Hebrew vocabulary index; thus, if you wish your baby's name to reflect a quality, like compassion, suggestions appear under that heading. The Hebrew spellings for the names in this chapter are based on Kolatch's research.*

Legend has it that name was given by some Danish Jews to honor the courage of King Christian X, who wore a yellow badge when the Nazis ordered Danish Jews to wear them.[9]

What you will find here, in addition to biblical names, are many traditional and modern Hebrew names, some Yiddish and a few Sephardic names. Also included are a handful of ethnic English-language names, which are associated with American *Yiddishkeit* and have experienced a renaissance in the last few years.

Many of the names that appear below are beautiful in both sound and meaning: Eliora (God is my light), Gila (joy), Rimona (pomegranate). Then again, some are simply melodic. For example, Aderet, which sounds lovely, means cape. Of course, the timeless name Leah means weariness. Unlike Americans, Israelis do not rule out names just because they have an unhappy literal meaning or biblical source. Hence the renaissance of the ill-fated Dina and the little-known Naphtali.

For many generations, children born on Jewish holidays were given names appropriate to the dates of their birth; thus babies were named Shabbatai, Pesach, and Yom Tov. It was a safe bet that anyone called Mordecai or Esther arrived during Purim. Those names have fallen far out of fashion with a majority of American Jews, but since they still have currency in Israel, some appear below.

Besides, fashion, by definition, changes with each generation if not every season. Names considered unthinkably old-fashioned only a decade ago have been reclaimed with a vengeance—just count the Sarahs and Aarons in the synagogue nursery school.

Speaking of Sarah, sources for girls' names reflect Judaism's undeniably patriarchal tradition. Thus there are fewer female prophets, warriors, and priests in the Bible after whom to name daughters. And the paucity of historical records about female Jewish scholars, leaders, and public figures before this century compounds the problem.

However, there is *yichus* (hereditary status) attached to certain women's names which date from more recent history. Emma, now a popular name, recalls modern heroines like political activist Goldman and poet Lazarus. And, of course, the greatest source of inspiration in naming any child may come from your own family saga. Thus, great-grandma Pearl, who put her children through college by working in a sweatshop where she was a union organizer, is no less lofty a namesake than Avital, wife of King David. And the names Pearl, Peninah, or Margalit all would honor her memory and serve your daughter well.

And finally, a baby's name can be either the excuse for an intergenerational and/or inter-*machatunim* (in-law) feud, or a means of knitting two families together. There is no reason why the baby can't have more than one Hebrew name: Sharon Esther Rivka's name honors her maternal great-grandmother and both her paternal great-aunts, for whom no one else is likely to be named. And think how impressive it will sound when she is called to the Torah with such an unforgettable, significant name.

When using these lists remember:

• The first version of each name is given in English, followed by alternative English spellings, followed by a transliteration of the Hebrew pronunciation if it differs significantly from the English. Unless otherwise noted, the translation is from Hebrew.

• All English versions of Hebrew names are transliterations, which means there is no exact correlate; Dina, Deena, Dena, Dinah are all correct. Choose the spelling you prefer, or make up your own.

• In most—though not all—Hebrew names, the accent falls on the second syllable. Thus, A*dam*. However, *Mal*kah. If you are unsure, ask someone who is more familiar with the language.

• A number of names are given with variations that change the meaning somewhat. Most common are the suffixes -i, -li, and -iel. For example, Ron, which means joy or song, becomes Roni (my joy), Ronli (joy is mine), Roniel (joy of God.)

• There is no "J" sound in Hebrew. Wherever a J appears, the Hebrew sound is "Y." Thus, Jonina is Yonina. In most cases, and especially where there is no common English version, such names are listed under "Y." However, where an English version is possible (Jasmine or Yasmin) both are given under the listing for "J."

A SON!

A

AARON, ARON, AHARON
Teaching, singing, shining, or mountain. The Aramaic root word means "messenger." Aharon was the older brother of Moses and Miriam. He was the first Israelite high priest and progenitor of all priests. Rabbinic tradition stresses his love of peace. He is said to have died at the age of 123 on Mount Horeb.

ABBA
Father. It's rather like naming your son "Daddy," but then again, Israeli statesman Abba Eban wears it well.

ABEL
Breath. The son of Adam and Eve, and the ill-fated brother of Cain.

ABIR
Strong.

ABNER, AVNER
Literally, father of light. It signifies brightness and light. Avner ben Ner was King Saul's uncle, and the commander of his army.

ABRAHAM, AVRAHAM
Father of a mighty nation. Abraham is known as the first Hebrew. His original name was Abram (Avram) which means exalted father. But when he accepted the covenant, by circumcising himself and establishing the practice among his people, the Hebrew letter hay, which appears twice in the unpronounceable name of God (Yud Hay Vav Hay) was added to his name. The

Arabic equivalent is Ali Baba. The patriarch Abraham is associated with *chesed,* loving-kindness, and hospitality. There are many nicknames associated with the name, including Avi, Abe, Abie. The Yiddish variations include Avrom and Avrumke.

ABSALOM, AVSHALOM

Father of peace. King David's third son. A later Absalom played a prominent part in the defense of Jerusalem against the Emperor Pompey.

ACHIYA

God is my brother. One of King David's warriors. The root/prefix, *achi,* or brother, gives rise to a whole list of names not in common use.

ADAM

Earth. From its Phoenician and Babylonian origins, mankind. The first man. A name not popular among Jews until modern times.

ADIN

Beautiful, pleasant, gentle. A biblical name, it has a few variations, including Adi, Adina, Adino, Adiv.

ADLAI

From the Aramaic, "refuge of God." The biblical Adlai was a shepherd.

ADMON

The name of a red peony that grows in the upper Galilee.

AKIBA, AKIVA

Akiva is derived from the same root as Jacob, Ya'akov, which means supplanter, or "held by the heel." Rabbi Akiva was a first century scholar and teacher, the founder of a famous academy. Common nicknames include Koby and Kivi.

ALEXANDER

Protector of men. Ever since the third century B.C.E., when Alexander the Great spared Jerusalem from harm, Jewish boys have been named in his honor. As the story goes, the high priest of Jerusalem was so grateful for Alexander's largess, he proclaimed that all Jewish males born in the city for a full year would bear the conqueror's name. Ever since, Alexander, in various languages and forms, has remained popular. Sander is the Yiddish equivalent. The Russian diminutive, Sasha, is currently enjoying popularity in America as a name for girls as well as boys. Other nicknames include Alex, Alexis, and Sandy.

ALON
Oak tree. A very popular name in Israel. One of the sons of Shimeon.

ALYAN
Heights.

AMAL
Work. A member of the tribe of Asher.

AMATZ, AMAZIAH
Strong, courageous.

AMI
My people. A popular Israeli name on its own, this root is found in many other names, a few of which follow.

AMICHAI
My people is alive.

AMIEL
God of my people.

AMIKAM
Nation arisen.

AMIN
Trustworthy.

AMIR
Strong.

AMIRAM
My people are lofty.

AMITAI
Truth, faithful. Amitai was the father of Jonah.

AMNON
Faithful. Amnon was the oldest son of David. Amnon of Mainz, a legendary figure and martyr of the tenth century C.E., is said to have composed the hymn *U'netanneh Tokef.*

AMOS
Burdened. A prophet who preached in the Northern Kingdom of Israel during the eighth century B.C.E. Social morality was his central theme. A very popular Israeli name.

AMRAM
A mighty nation. Amram was the father of Moses, Miriam and Aaron. The *Mahzor de Rav Amram,* written during the ninth century C.E., is one of the oldest surviving prayer books; the Gaon, as he was called, established the order of the siddur used to this day.

ARIEL
Lion of God. Also a poetic name for the city of Jerusalem. Ari and Arik are diminutives.

ARNON
Roaring stream. In the Bible, the Arnon was a stream in the Moab.

ARYEH
Lion. The name Aryeh appears in the Bible, once as an army officer. Ari, now a popular name in its own right in Israel, is a diminutive of Aryeh.

ASA
Healer. A king of Judea.

ASHER
Blessed, fortunate. Asher was the son of Jacob and Zilpah, and

the leader of one of the twelve tribes of Israel. Anshel is the Yiddish.

AVI
Father. A diminutive of Avraham, but also used as a name on its own, this is the prefix/root for a great many names, some of which follow.

AVICHAI
My father lives.

AVIDAN
Father of justice or God is just.

AVIEL
God is my father.

AVIEZER
Father helper.

AVIGDOR
Father protector. Popular in Israel.

AVIMELECH
Father king.

AVINOAM
Father of delight.

AVISHAI
In Aramaic, "gift of God." A grandson of the biblical Jesse.

AVISHALOM
Father of peace.

AVIV
Spring.

AZI
Strong.

AZRIEL
God is my help.

B

BARAK
Lightning. A biblical soldier during the reign of Deborah.

BARAM
Son of the nation.

BARUCH
Blessed. Baruch was friend and secretary to the prophet Jeremiah. The Yiddish version, Bendit, is actually based on the name Benedict. The philosopher Baruch Spinoza (1632–1677) was known as Benedict de Spinoza.

BEN-AMI
Son of my people. The prefix *ben* is attached to a number of words and names.

BENJAMIN, BINYAMIN
Son of my right hand. Benjamin was the youngest of Jacob's sons, his second child with Rachel, who died giving birth to him. He was the only brother of eleven who did not participate in Joseph's sale into slavery and was honored by having the Holy Temple built on territory allotted to his tribe.

BEN-ZION
Son of Zion. Benzi is a popular nickname.

BERYL
A Yiddish diminutive for bear. Also Ber. The Hebrew equivalent is Dov.

BOAZ
Strength and swiftness. The great-grandfather of King David, Boaz was a wealthy, land-owning Bethlehemite who married Ruth. (Ruth 2:4)

C

CALEB, CALEV
Heart, also dog. One of the twelve spies sent by Moses to reconnoiter Canaan. Only he and Joshua brought back a favorable report, for which they were allowed to enter the promised land.

CHAIM, HAYYIM
Life.

D

DAN
Judge. Dan was the fifth son of Jacob, and first-born of Bilhah, Rachel's maidservant. Dani is a variant.

DANIEL
God is my judge. The Book of Ezekiel mentions a pious and wise Daniel, who predated Moses. Daniel, the hero of the book of Daniel, was known as an interpreter of visions. He predicted the future triumph of a Messianic kingdom.

DAVID
Beloved. David was the shepherd anointed by the prophet Samuel as the future king. His career began with the killing of Goliath; his popularity aroused King Saul's jealousy. King first of Judah and later of Israel, David created a loose national union of the tribes, eventually making Jerusalem his capital. One of the most beloved figures in Judaism, it is believed that the Messiah will be one of David's descendants. Since Talmudic times, his name has been a favorite.

DEROR, DERORI, DROR
Freedom. Also, a bird. A popular Israeli name.

DEVIR
Holy place. In the Bible, Devir was a king of Eglon.

DOR
A generation.

DORAN
Gift.

DOTAN
Law. In the Bible, Dotan was a place in Palestine, north of Samaria.

DOV
Bear. Dubi is a popular Israeli nickname. (See also Beryl.)

E

EFRAYIM, EFRAIM, EPHREM, EPHRAIM
Fruitful. Efrayim was Joseph's son and Jacob's grandson. His name is mentioned in the traditional Friday night blessing over sons.

EFRON
A bird.

ELAZAR
God has helped. Aaron's third son, Elazar became the high priest. There have been many famous Elazars throughout history, including Eleazar ben Jair, a commander in Masada, whose eloquence persuaded the city's defenders that suicide was preferable to surrender or defeat.

ELI, ELY
Ascend. In the Bible, Eli was a high priest of the prophet Samuel.

ELIAKIM
God established.

ELIEZER
My God has helped. The name Eliezer appears three times in the Bible: Abraham's steward, Moses' son, and a prophet in the time of Jehosaphat. The name belonged to three great Talmudic scholars and many great German rabbis.

ELIHU

He is my God. The name Elihu appears several times in the Bible, once as a young friend of Job.

ELIJAH, ELIAHU

The Lord is my God. Elijah was a prophet who lived in the time of Ahab and Jezebel during the ninth century B.C.E. and led the fight against the cult of Baal. He ascended to heaven in a chariot of fire, but according to tradition, did not die and continues to accompany Israel in her exile. He is often disguised as a poor beggar. Elijah's presence is invoked during Passover, and at circumcisions. He is viewed as a herald of the Messiah.

The name has many translations: in German it is Elias; in French, Elie; in Italian, Elia. In English, Eliot, Ellis, and Elias are all based on the name Elijah. Elya is a common Israeli nickname.

ELISHA

God is my salvation. Elisha the prophet succeeded Elijah. In Second Kings, there are miraculous stories about his long life.

ELKANAH

God brought.

EMANUEL, EMMANUEL

God is with us.

ENOCH

Dedicated. Enoch was Cain's son, born after Abel died.

ESHKOL

A cluster of grapes. In Hebrew letters, Eshkol signifies a gathering of scholars. Levi Eshkol was Israeli prime minister from 1963 to 1969.

ETAN, EYTAN

Strong.

EVEN

Stone. Eben and Eban are based on this name.

EYAL, AYAL
A stag.

EZEKIEL
God will strengthen. Ezekiel was a prophet who lived during the sixth century B.C.E., at the time of the end of the first Temple. Ezekiel's description of the Divine Throne was the major text for Jewish mysticism (*Ma'aseh Merkavah*).

EZRA, EZRI
Help. A priest and scribe of the fifth century B.C.E. who led a return from Babylon to Jerusalem, where he became a key figure in the reconstruction of the Temple and religious life. He has been compared in importance with Moses for his observance and instruction in Torah, and for having introduced the square Hebrew alphabet.

G

GABRIEL, GAVRIEL
God is my strength. Gabriel is the angel that visited Daniel. In Israel, the diminutive Gabi is also used as a full name. Gavirol is a Sephardic variation, Gavri is a nickname.

GAD
Happy. Gad was one of Jacob's sons. Also, Gadi, a diminutive.

GAL, GALI
A wave or a mountain. Also, Galya.

GAMALIEL, GAMLIEL
God is my reward. The name of many Talmudic scholars.

GAN
Garden.

GARON
A threshing floor.

GEDALIA, GEDALIAH, GEDALIAHU
God is great. Gedaliah was a governor of Judea.

GERSHOM, GERSON
I was a stranger there. Moses named his older son Gershom, referring to the experience in Egypt. The name has served many teachers, including Gershom Scholem, the great twentieth-century scholar of mystical Judaism.

GIBOR
Strong, hero.

GIDEON
A mighty warrior. Gideon was a warrior-hero, reputed to have fathered seventy sons. Gidi is a popular nickname.

GIL, GILL, GILI, GILLI
Joy. Gili means "my joy."

GILAD, GILEAD, GILADI
From a place name, a mountain range east of the Jordan river.

GUR, GURI, GURIEL
Respectively, young lion, my young lion, and God is my lion. Guryon is another variation.

H

HADAR
Adornment. A biblical king.

HANAN
Grace or gracious. A shortened form of Yohanan.

HAREL
Mountain of God. A biblical place name.

HASKEL, HASKELL
Yiddish form of Ezekiel.

HERSCH, HERSH
In Yiddish, a deer. The diminutives and variations of Hersch are numerous: Herschel, Hesh, Heshel, Herzl, Hirsh, Hirsch. (See Tzvi, the Hebrew equivalent.)

HILLEL
Praised. Hillel became a popular name in honor of the great Palestinian scholar born in Babylon in 75 B.C.E. Hilly is a popular nickname.

HIRAM
Noble born. Hiram was king of Tyre, c. 969-936 B.C.E. He helped in the planning, building and equipping of the Temple in Jerusalem.

HOD
Splendor, vigor. Hod was a member of the tribe of Asher. Popular in Israel.

I

IRA
Descendants.

ISAAC, ITZAK, YITZHAK
Laughter. Isaac, one of the three patriarchs, was the son of Abraham and Sarah, born to them very late in life. He was the first Jew to be circumcised on the eighth day of life. The story of his binding, the *Akeda,* is one of the most provocative and powerful of all biblical stories. The name has remained popular, serving, among others, Isaac Luria, the Safed mystic who established the Lurianic Kabbalah. There are many nicknames: Ike, Issa, and Yitz among them.

ISAIAH, YISHAYAHU
God is salvation. Isaiah was a prophet in Jerusalem in the 700s B.C.E. Isa is a popular nickname.

ISRAEL, YISRAEL, YISROEL
Wrestler with God. The name given to Jacob after he wrestled with the angel, which became a synonym for the Jewish people.

ISSACHAR
There is a reward. Issachar was the son of Jacob and Leah, one of the leaders of the twelve tribes of Israel.

ITAI, ITTAI
Friendly. Itai was one of David's warriors.

ITIEL
God is with me. Itiel was a member of the tribe of Benjamin.

ITTAMAR
Island of palm. A name that signifies gracefulness. One of the sons of Aaron. Ismar is an Ashkenazic transliteration of the name.

*J**

JACOB, YACOV, YA'ACOV
Held by the heel, supplanter. The third of the patriarchs, his name was changed to Israel after his wrestling match with the angel. There are many nicknames and derivatives of Jacob, from James to Jack to Jake to Yankele.

JARED, YARED
To descend.

JEDEDIAH, YEDAIAH
The name of two priestly ancestral houses mentioned in the book of Nehemiah.

JEREMIAH, JEREMY, YIR'MIAHU
God will uplift. Jeremiah began to prophesy around 625 B.C.E. His gloomy forecasts aroused resentment and he spent many years in jail.

JESSE, YISHAI
Gift. Jesse was the father of David, the grandson of Boaz and Ruth.

** What commonly appears in English as "J" is pronounced "Y" in Hebrew; thus, Jacob is Yacov. Many names that appear anglicized as J-names are listed below, under Y. The names that appear here, however, are well-known in English.*

JETHRO, YITRO
Abundance, riches. Father of Zipporah, and Moses' father-in-law, Jethro was a Midianite priest.

JOEL, YOEL
God is willing. Joel is one of the twelve minor prophets who preached in Judea.

JONAH, YONAH
Dove. Jonah was the prophet who traveled inside a whale. A complex biblical character.

JONATHAN, YONATAN
God has given. Jonathan was the son of Saul. His friendship with David is one of the most moving biblical stories. Yoni is a popular Israeli nickname.

JORDAN, YARDEN
Descend. Yori is a popular Israeli nickname.

JOSEPH, YOSEF
God will increase. The son of Jacob and Rachel, almost 25 percent of Genesis is devoted to Joseph's story. A dreamer as well as a shrewd politician, his name has been a favorite throughout Jewish history. Jose, the Aramaic form of the name, was popular in Talmudic times.

JOSHUA, YEHOSHUA
The Lord is my salvation. Joshua succeeded Moses as the leader of the Hebrews to the land of Israel. Moses changed his successor's name from Hoshua by adding a *yud*, one of the letters of God's name; thus, Yehoshua.

JOSIAH, YOSHIAHU
God has protected. Son of Amnon, Josiah became a king of Judah at the age of eight.

JUDAH, YEHUDA
Praise. Judah was the fourth son of Jacob and Leah. In the Joseph story, he plays a special role, with Reuben and Benjamin,

as a spokesman for his brother. Judah received special blessings from his father, Jacob. Yehuda is the source of the words Judaism, Jewish, and Jew. There have been many famous Judahs, including the Hebrew poet Judah Halevi.

K

KADMEIL
God is the ancient One.

KALIL
Crown or wreath.

KANIEL
A reed or stalk. Since in Aramaic, Kaniel means spear, the name connotes strength.

KATRIEL
Crown of the Lord.

KENAN
To acquire. A nephew of Abraham in the Bible.

KOBY
A nickname for Jacob.

KORE, KORIE
Quail, or to call.

L

LABAN
White. Laban was Rebecca's brother, the father of matriarchs Rachel and Leah, grandfather of the twelve tribes of Israel. Nonetheless, an unsavory character.

LAVI
Lion.

LAZAR, LEYZER
A Greek form of Eliezer and a popular Yiddish name.

LEOR
I have light.

LEV
Heart in Hebrew. Lion in Yiddish, where Label is a nickname.

LEVI
Attendant. The name Levi signifies devotion. In the Bible, he was the third of Jacob's sons born to Leah. His descendants became the Levites, the priests in the Temple.

LIRON.
My song.

LOTAN
Protect. Popular in Israel.

M

MAIMON
Aramaic for luck or good fortune. The philosopher Moses ben Maimon, known as Maimonides, is the most illustrious bearer of the name.

MALACHI
Messenger or angel. The last of the prophets.

MALKAM
God is their King.

MATTATHIAS, MATTITYAHU
Gift from God. A name linked to Chanukah, Mattathias was the father of Judah Maccabee, and the patriarch of the Hasmonean dynasty. Common nicknames include Matt, Matti, Matia.

MEGED
Goodness, sweetness.

MEIR, MEYER
One who shines.

MENACHEM

Comforter. A biblical king known for his cruelty, Menachem was the name given to boys born on the 9th of Av, the day of mourning for the destruction of the Temple. Yiddish derivatives include Mendel and Mannes.

MENASSEH, MANASSEH, MENASHE

Causing to forget. The older of Joseph's sons, Menasseh and his brother Ephraim are mentioned in the Shabbat blessing over sons.

MERON

Troops. Also a town in Israel; popular name there today.

MICAH

Who is like God. Micah was a prophet in Judah during the eighth century B.C.E., who denounced oppression by the ruling classes.

MICHAEL

Who is like God. Michael was the angel closest to God, and God's messenger. Variations on Michael include: Mike, Mickey, Mitchell, and the Russian, Misha.

MIRON

A holy place.

MORDECAI, MORDECHAI

Persian for warrior or warlike. Mordecai was Queen Esther's cousin, who advised her on the saving of the Jews. It was a name commonly given boys born during Purim. Yiddish nicknames include Mottel, Motke, and Mordke. Motti is the Israeli pet name.

MORI

My teacher. Also a variation on Morrey, a nickname for Maurice or Morris, which is an anglicization of Moses.

MOSES, MOSE, MOSHE

Saved from the water. Also Egyptian for son or child. The

leader and teacher who brought the Israelites out of bondage in Egypt. Variations on the name include Moss, Moise (French) and Moishe (Yiddish). Jewish immigrants to America named their Moishes Milton, Melvin, Morris, Maurice.

N

NAAMAN
Sweet, beautiful. A biblical general.

NACHMAN
Comforter.

NACHUM, NAHUM
Comforted. A prophet in the seventh century B.C.E.

NADAV
Benefactor.

NAMIR
Leopard.

NAOR
Light.

NAPHTALI, NAFTALI
To wrestle. Jacob's sixth son by Bilhah.

NATHAN, NATAN
He gave. Nathan was one of the minor prophets, who, together with Zadok the priest, anointed Solomon king. In Yiddish, the name is Nusan.

NATHANIEL
Gift of God. Nathaniel was the fourth son of Jesse, and David's brother.

NAVON
Wise.

NEHEMIAH, NECHEMYA
Comforted of the Lord. Nehemiah served as a governor of Judea, and was involved in rebuilding the walls of Jerusalem.

NIR, NIREL, NIRIA, NIRIEL
Plow or plowed field. Niriel means the tilled field of the Lord.

NISSAN
Flight, also emblem. Nissan is also the name of the lunar month in which Passover falls. Nisi is a popular nickname.

NISSIM
Miracles. A popular Sephardic name in Israel.

NIV
Aramaic and Arabic for speech.

NOAH
Rest or peace. Noah and his family survived the great flood sent by God to punish an evil world because he was the only righteous man of his time. Noah was the first to plant a vineyard. It is pronounced Noach in Hebrew.

NOAM
Sweetness, friendship.

NUR, NURI
Of Aramaic origin, fire. Also Nuria, Nurieh, and Nuriel, which means fire of the Lord.

O

OBADIAH, OVADIAH, OVED
Servant of God. Obadiah was one of the twelve minor prophets and the author of the Bible's shortest book. Another biblical Oved was King David's grandfather.

OFER
A young deer.

OMRI
From the Arabic for to live long. Omri was a king in Israel during the 800s B.C.E.

OREN, ORIN, ORRIN, ORON
Fir tree, cedar. A popular Israeli name.

OZ, OZNI
Strength, hearing. Ozni was a grandson of Jacob.

P

PALTI, PALTIEL, PILTAI
My deliverance. A common name in the Bible. Palti was Michal's second husband, Piltai a member of a priestly family.

PERETZ
Burst forth.

PESACH
Pass over. A name often given boys born during the holiday of Pesach.

PINCHAS, PINCUS
Dark-complexioned. Pinchas (Phineas in Greek) was a priest, a grandson of Aaron.

R

RAANAN
Fresh, luxuriant.

RACHIM, RACHAMIM
Compassion. A common name among Sephardic Jews.

RANEN, RANON
To sing.

RAPHAEL
God has healed. Raphael is one of the four archangels. According to the Talmud, he was one of the three angels who visited

Abraham, and he is associated with healing. Also spelled Rafael and Refael; Rafi is a popular nickname.

RAVID
Ornament.

RAVIV
Rain or dew.

RAZ, RAZI, RAZIEL
From the Aramaic for secret.

REUBEN, REUVEN
Behold, a son. Jacob and Leah's first son.

RIMON
Pomegranate.

RON, RONEL, RONI, RONLI
Song and joy, in various settings.

S

SAADIAH, SAADYA
Aramaic for Ezra, meaning God's help. Saadiah ben Joseph was a great Egyptian-born scholar of the ninth century. A popular Sephardic name.

SAMSON, SHIMSHON
Sun, signifying strength. Strongman Samson, most famous for his betrayal by Delilah, was from the tribe of Dan.

SAMUEL, SH'MUEL
God has heard. Samuel was the son of Hannah, raised by the priest Eli. He was instrumental in the creation of a centralized monarchy in the eleventh century B.C.E., and as prophet and judge, anointed King Saul and later King David. Samuel was the last of the Judges.

SAUL, SHA'UL
Borrowed. Saul was the first king of Israel, from the tribe of Benjamin.

SETH, SHET
Appointed. The name comes from the line "Because God appointed me another seed beside Abel." Seth was Adam's son, born after Abel's death.

SHAI
Gift.

SHALOM, SHLOMO, SHOLOM, SHLOMI
Peace.

SHAMIR
Strong.

SHRAGA
Light, in Aramaic.

SIMCHA
Joy. Also, a girl's name.

SIMON, SIMEON, SHIMON, SHIMEON
To hear. Shimon was the second son born to Jacob and Leah. (Simon is the Greek version.) Simi is a popular nickname for Shimon in Israel.

SIVAN
The seventh month, whose symbol in the horoscope is Gemini.

SOLOMON
Peace. Solomon, the son of David and Bathsheba, built the first Temple. He is the poet who wrote Song of Songs, Proverbs and Ecclesiastes. His reputation for wisdom—especially in resolving the case where two women claimed the same child as their own—is enshrined in the adjective solomonic.

T

TABBAI
From the Aramaic word, good. Names like Tov, Tovi, and Tavi share the root and meaning.

TAL, TALOR
Dew, dew of light. The root is also the basis for a girl's name.

TAMIR
Tall, like the tamar or palm tree.

TIMUR
Tall, also derived from the word for palm tree.

TIVON
Student of nature.

TOBIAH, TUV'YA
The Lord is my God. Toby is the popular nickname.

TZEVI
Deer. Also spelled Tzvi, Zevi, and Zvi. Very popular in Israel.

U

URI, URIEL
From the root word light. According to *Midrash Rabbah,* Uriel is one of the four angels who resides around God's throne.

W

WOLF, WOLFE
Yiddish for wolf, where variants include Vulf and Velvel. (See Ze'ev.)

Y

YAKIR
Beloved.

YALON
He will rest. A son of Caleb.

YAMIR
To change.

YANIR
He will plow.

YARON
To sing.

YAVNIEL
God will build.

YEFET
Beautiful. Also spelled Yafet, Yaphet. Yefet was one of Noah's sons.

YEHIEL
May God live. Yehiel was a musician in the court of King David.

YIGAL
He will redeem. Popular in Israel.

YOAV
God is father. King David's nephew and an officer in his army.

YOCHANAN
God is gracious. There are more than fifty Yochanons in the Talmud.

YORAM
God is exalted.

YORAN
To sing.

Z

ZACH
Pure and clean.

ZACHARY, ZACHARIAH

Remembering the Lord. The name of one of the minor prophets, and of a king of Judah and a king of Israel. Nicknames include Zack and Zeke.

ZALMAN

Yiddish for Shlomo.

ZAMIR

Song, also nightingale.

ZAVDI, ZAVDIEL

My gift, gift of God. An officer in David's army.

ZEBULON, ZEVULON

To exalt or honor. Zevulon was the sixth son of Jacob and Leah.

ZEDEKIAH

God is righteousness. A king of Judah.

ZE'EV, ZEV, ZEVI, ZEVIEL

Wolf in Hebrew. (See Wolf.) Very popular in Israel.

ZEPHANIAH

God has treasured. A seventh century B.C.E. prophet, Zephaniah belonged to the family of Judah.

ZERACH

Light rising.

ZION, TZION

Excellent, a sign. The name of the whole Jewish people, and of a mountain in Jerusalem.

ZIV, ZIVI

To shine.

ZOHAR

Light, brilliance.

ZUSHYE, ZUSYA

Yiddish for sweet.

A Daughter!

A

ABIGAIL, AVIGAIL
Father's joy. Abigail was an early supporter of King David, even before she became his wife. She was known for her beauty, wisdom and powers of prophecy.

ABIRA
Strong.

ABRA
From the Hebrew root Abba or father. A diminutive of Abraham.

ADA, ADI
Ornament.

ADENA, ADINA
Noble or adorned, gentle.

ADERET
A cape or outer garment.

ADIRA
Strong.

ADIVA
Gracious, pleasant.

ADRA
From the Aramaic, glory or majesty.

ADVA
An Aramaic name that means wave or ripple.

AHARONA
Feminine version of Aaron, which means teaching or singing. Variations include, Arona, Arni, Arnina, Arnit, Arninit.

AHAVA
Love, beloved.

ALEEZA, ALIZA, ALITZA
Joy or joyous one.

ALEXANDRA
Feminine of the Greek ruler Alexander. See "Alexander" for a full explanation of the name. Also, Queen Salome Alexandra was a ruler of Judea.

ALIYA, ALIYAH
To go up. When one is called up to the Torah in the synagogue, one is given an aliyah. Also, moving to Israel is called making aliyah. Aliya is sometimes given to daughters by refusenik parents in the Soviet Union.

ALMA
Maiden. In Spanish, it means soul.

ALONA
Oak tree. Alon is a popular boy's name.

ALUMA, ALUMIT
Girl or maiden.

AMALIA
The work of the Lord.

AMIRA
Speech. Ear of corn.

ANNA, ANN
These and many more (Annette, Annie, Anita, Anya) are all forms of the biblical name Hannah. Anna is the Hellenized version.

ARELLA
Angel, messenger.

ARIEL, ARIELLA
Lion or lioness of God.

ARMONA, ARMONIT
Castle or palace.

ARNA, ARNIT
Cedar.

ARNONA, ARNONIT
From arnon, a roaring stream.

ARZA, ARZIT
Cedar beams.

ASHIRA
Wealthy.

ATARA, ATARET
Crown.

ATIRA
Prayer.

AVIELLA
God is my father.

AVITAL
Dew of my father. A wife of King David.

AVIVA
Spring. A popular Israeli name. Avivit and Avivi mean spring-like. Avivit is also the word for lilac.

AVODA
Work.

AYALA
Deer or gazelle.

AZA, AZAH, AZIZA
Strong.

B

BAILA, BAYLE
Yiddish form of Bilhah, one of the four mothers of the tribes of Israel. The Latin root means beautiful. Bella and Belle are derivatives.

BAT-AMI
Daughter of my people.

BATSHEVA
Daughter of the oath. Batsheva was one of David's wives, known for her beauty. Solomon was their second son. Batshuva is a variant spelling and Basha is a diminutive.

BATYA
Daughter of God.

BENYAMINA
The feminine form of Benjamin.

BERIT, B'ERIT
A well.

BERURIAH, BERURYAH
Pure or clean. Beruriah was the daughter of Rabbi Haninah ben Teradyon, and the wife of Rabbi Meir. She lived in the second century C.E. and was renowned for moral stature and intellectual incisiveness. She is the only woman in Talmudic literature whose views were taken seriously by her contemporaries.

BINA
Understanding, intelligence.

BIRA
Fortress.

BLUMA, BLUME
Yiddish, flower.

BONA
Builder.

BRACHA
Blessing.

BRINA
With joy. Based on the Slavic Bronia.

C

CARMEL, CARMELLE, CARMELA, CARMELIT
Vineyard. A very popular Israeli name with many variations: Carma, Carmit, Carmia.

CARNA, CARNIT
Horn. Carniella means horn of God.

CHAVA
Eve. Mother of life.

CHAYA
Life.

CLARA
Yiddish, meaning clean.

D

DAFNA
Laurel.

DALIA, DALIT
Branch.

DANIELLA, DANIELLE
God is my judge. The feminine version of Daniel has many derivatives: Dania, Dani, Danya, Danit.

DANYA
Feminine of Dan.

DAVIDA, DAVITA
The feminine of David, meaning beloved or friend. Nickname, Davi.

DEBORAH, DEBRA, DEVORAH, DEVRA
To speak kindly, or a swarm of bees. Devorah was a prophetess and judge who led a revolt against a Canaanite king. Her composition, the "Song of Deborah," is one of the oldest known Hebrew poems.

DEENA, DENA, DINA, DINAH
Judgment. Deena was the daughter of Jacob and Leah.

DEGANIA
Corn. Also the first kibbutz.

DELILA
Poor or hair. Delila was a Philistine woman, Samson's mistress.

DERORA, DRORA
Freedom.

DIZA, DITZA
Joy.

DODI, DODIE
Beloved, friend.

DORIT
Of this era. Very popular in Israel.

DORONIT
Aramaic for gift.

DORYA
Generation of God.

DOVA, DOVEVA, DOVIT
Bear.

E

EDNA

Delight, pleasure. Edna appears in the book of Tobit, in the Apocrypha.

EFRAT

Honored, distinguished.

EFRONA

A song bird.

ELANA

Oak tree. Ilana is a variant English spelling.

ELIANA

God has answered me.

ELINOAR

God of my youth.

ELIORA

God is my light.

ELISHEVA

God is my oath. Elisheva was Aaron's wife, the matriarch of the priestly caste. The Hellenized form is Elizabeth, which has many nicknames and derivatives: Ella, Elisa, Eliza, Elise, Elsie, Betsy, Liz, Libby, Betty, Elyssa.

Elisheva Bikhowsky (1888–1949) was a Russian-born poet who settled in Israel in 1925, where she published in Hebrew.

EMANUELLA

God is with us.

EMMA

Originally from the Teutonic for grandmother or big one, the name was popular among Jewish immigrants to America at the turn of the century including the Russian-born anarchist writer and organizer Emma Goldman, and the poet Emma Lazarus. The name Emma is again popular in America but is not used in Israel.

EMUNA
Faith.

ESTHER, ESTER
From the Persian for star. Esther is the heroine of the story of Purim. She, with help from her cousin Mordechai, averted the annihilation of the Jews in her community. The Hebrew name for Esther is Hadassah, which means myrtle. Variations include Esta, Essie, Estelle and Estella. Etti is a popular Israeli nickname.

EVA, EVE, CHAVA
Life. According to Genesis, Eve was the first woman, the mother of all human life.

EZRAELA
God is my help. The feminine for Ezra.

F

FRIEDA, FRAYDE, FREYDEL
Yiddish for joy.

G

GABRIELLA, GAVRIELLA
God is my strength. The feminine version of Gabriel; nicknames include Gabi and Gavi.

GALI, GALIT
Fountain or spring.

GALYA
God's hill.

GAMLIELA, GAMLIELLE
Feminine forms of Gamliel.

GANIT
Garden.

GARNIT
Granary.

GAVRILLA
Heroine, strong.

GAYORA
Valley of light.

GAZIT
Hewn stone.

GEULA
Redemption.

GILA, GEELA
Joy. Gilana and Gilat also mean joy. Gilia, a variant, means my joy is in the Lord.

GILADA
My joy is forever.

GINA, GINAT
Garden.

GITA, GITTLE
Yiddish, good one. (See Tova.)

GIVA, GIVONA
Hill.

GOLDA, GOLDE
Yiddish for golden. The Hebrew is Zahava.

GURIT
Cub.

*H**

HADARA, HADURA
Splendid.

**Nearly all these names begin with the sound "ch."*

HADASS, HADASSAH
Myrtle tree, which is a symbol of victory. Esther's Hebrew name. Nicknames include Dass and Dasi.

HAGIT
Festive, joyous.

HAMUDA
Precious.

HANNAH
Gracious, merciful. Hannah was the mother of Samuel, wife of Elkanah. Despairing because she was barren, Hannah prayed at the temple of Shiloh, where she pledged that if granted a son she would dedicate him to God's service. She gave birth to Samuel, which means "God listened." The Christian Bible refers to Hannah as Anna.

HASIA
Protected of the Lord.

HASIDA
Pious one. Also, stork.

HAVIVA
Beloved.

HEDVA
Joy.

HEDYA
Voice of the Lord.

HEFZIBA, CHEFTZEEBA
My desire.

HEMDA
Precious.

—

HERZLIA
Yiddish for deer. The feminine version of a masculine name, it is also the name of an Israeli city. The name recalls Zionist leader Theodor Herzl.

HILA, HILLA
Praise. Hillela is the feminine version of Hillel, which also means praise.

HINDA
Yiddish for deer.

I

ILANA, ILANIT
Oak tree. Elana is a variant English spelling.

IRIT
Daffodil. Popular in Israel.

ISAACA
Laughter. The feminine of Isaac.

ISRAELA, ISA
The name of the people, almost always used in the diminutive, Isa.

ITI, ITTI
With me.

J

JACOBA, YACOVA
To supplant. The feminine of Yacov.

JASMINE, YASMIN
The flower.

JEMINA, YEMINA
Right handed.

JESSIE, JESSICA, YISKA
God's grace.

JOHANNA, YOCHANA
God is glorious. Feminine of Jochanan.

JONINA, YONINA
Dove.

JOSEPHA, YOSEFA
God will increase. The feminine of Joseph.

JUDITH, YEHUDIT
Praise. In an Apocryphal story, Judith was the heroine who saved Jerusalem by pretending to defect to the camp of General Holofernes, where she beheaded him while he slept.

K

KADIA, KADYA
Pitcher.

KALANIT
Anemone.

KANARIT, KANIT
Songbird.

KARNA, KARNIT
Horn, as in ram's horn. A related name very popular in Israel is Keren.

KAYLA
Yiddish form of Kelila. (See below.)

KELILA
A crown of laurel, symbolizing victory.

KETZIA
Fragrant. One of Job's daughters.

KINNERET
Hebrew name of the Sea of Galilee. Also, harp.

KIRYA
Village.

L

LAILA, LEILA, LILA
Night.

LEAH, LEA
In Hebrew it means weariness but in Assyrian it means mistress or ruler. The daughter of Laban, and Jacob's first wife, Leah is one of the four matriarchs of Judaism. She gave birth to six sons: Reuben, Simeon, Levi, Judah, Issachar, Zebulon, and one daughter, Dinah. Her marriage was the result of her father's trickery, substituting her for her sister, Rachel.

LEEBA, LIBA, LIEBE
Yiddish for beloved. In Israel, the name also refers to the Hebrew root lev, which means heart.

LEORA, LIORA
Light, my light.

LEVANA, LIVANA
Moon, or white. Popular among Sephardic Israelis.

LEVONA
Spice or incense.

LILY
Not a Hebrew name, popular name among American Jewish immigrants in the early twentieth century.

LIVIA, LIVYA
A crown. When the accent falls on the last syllable, Livia means lioness. Also spelled Levia.

M

MAGDA
A high tower.

MAHIRA, MEHIRA
Energetic.

MALKAH
Queen. A popular Sephardic name. (See Regina.)

MARGALIT
Pearl. (See Peninah.)

MARNI, MARNINA
Rejoice.

MARVA
Mint.

MAXIMA
Enchanter.

MERI
Rebellious.

MICHAELA
Who is like God. Feminine of Michael, the name of one of the archangels. Mia is a nickname.

MICHAL
A contraction of Michaela. Michal was the youngest daughter of King Saul, and wife of King David. At one point, Michal saved David from Saul's wrath.

MILI
Who is for me?

MIRA
Light. Feminine of Meir. Miera and Meera are variations.

MIRIAM, MIRYAM
Sorrow or bitterness in Hebrew. In Chaldean, mistress of the sea. Miriam was a prophetess, singer and dancer, the sister of Moses and Aaron. Nicknames include: Mim, Mindy, Minna, Mira, Mirel, Miri, and Mirit.

MIRIT
Sweet wine.

MORIAH, MORIT
Teacher.

N

NAAMAH, NAAMIT
Pleasant, beautiful.

NAAVA
Beautiful.

NADYA
From dowry. Used in Israel.

NAOMI
Beautiful, pleasant. In the Book of Ruth, Naomi was Elimelech's wife and the mother-in-law of Ruth. She encouraged Ruth to marry her kinsman, Boaz.

NASIA, NASYA
Miracle of God.

NATANIA
Gift of God, feminine of Nathan.

NEDIVA
Noble, generous.

NEHAMA
Comfort.

NEIMA
Pleasant.

NESYA
Yiddish for Nissan, the month of flowers.

NETA, NETIA
A plant.

NETANYA
Gift of God.

NILI
A plant.

NINA
In Hebrew, the word for granddaughter.

NIRA
Light.

NIRIT
A flowering plant.

NITZA
Bud.

NOA
Tremble, shake. A biblical name popular in Israel today.

NOGA
Morning light.

NURIT
Buttercup.

O

ODELIA
I will praise God.

ODERA
Plow.

OPHIRA
Gold.

OPHRAH, OFRA
Young deer.

ORA, ORAH
Light.

ORLI, ORLIT
My light.

ORNA
Cedar.

P

PAZIT
Gold.

PENINAH, PENINIT
Pearl or coral. Elkanah's second wife. (See Margalit.)

PUAH
A midwife during the Egyptian captivity, Puah and her colleague Shifra disobeyed Pharaoh's order to kill all male Hebrews at birth.

R

RACHEL
A ewe, symbol of gentility and purity. Rachel was the best-loved wife of Jacob, who gave birth to Joseph and Benjamin. She is described as "shapely and beautiful" but suffered barrenness for many years. The traditional site of her tomb near Bethlehem was venerated from at least the fourth century C.E. There have been many renowned Rachels, among them Rabbi Akiva's wife, a wealthy woman who, against her father's wishes, married the poor and at the time unlearned Akiva, and encouraged his studies.

RAISA, RAIZEL
Yiddish for Rose.

RAKEFET
Cyclamen, a beautiful flower common in Israel.

RANANA
Fresh.

RANIT, RANITA
Joy or song.

RAPHAELA
God has healed. Feminine of Raphael.

RAYNA, REYNA
Yiddish for pure or clean.

RAZI, RAZIA, RAZIELLA
Aramaic for secret. Razili means my secret.

REBECCA, REBEKAH, RIVKA
Beautiful, or to tie or bind. The wife of Isaac, mother of Jacob and Esau, Rebecca was the strong-willed matriarch who masterminded Jacob's deception of his father to gain the family blessing. Nicknames include Becky and Rikki.

REGINA
Sephardic name meaning queen. Malkah in Hebrew.

RIMONA
Pomegranate.

RINA
Joy or song. Renana, Renanit are variations.

RIVA
Young girl, also a diminutive of Rebecca.

RONA, RONI, RONIT, RONIA
Joy or song.

ROSE, ROSA
The translation of the popular Hebrew name Shoshana.

Rose has been a popular name in many languages, including English, Yiddish, Ladino, and Hebrew. (See Raisel, Susan, Varda, Vered.)

Rose Schneiderman (1882–1972) was an American labor organizer and president of the Women's Trade Union League from 1918 to 1949.

RUTH

Friendship. The daughter-in-law of Naomi, who chose to stay with Naomi and the Jewish people after the death of her husband. Ruth is considered the model of the righteous convert to Judaism. She is the ancestor of David, from whose line—says the tradition—will come the Messiah.

S

SAMANTHA

Samantha is often given in memory of a grandfather Samuel, although there is no real connection between the two names.

SARA, SARAH

Princess. Sarah is the first Jewish woman. The wife of Abraham, she gave birth to Isaac at the age of ninety. She was known for her beauty, and her hospitality. Nicknames include: Sari, Sarene, Sarina, Sarit. Yiddish versions include: Sorale, Soralie. Sadie, once a common Jewish-American variation, is making a comeback in the United States.

SASHA

Variation on Alexandra, used as a proper name.

SERAFINA

To burn. From the same root as the biblical seraphim, angels surrounding God's throne.

SHALVIA, SYLVIA

Peace, tranquillity.

SHARON
A variety of rose in Israel. King Solomon sang of the roses of Sharon.

SHAYNA, SHAINE
Yiddish for beautiful.

SHELI, SHELLI
Mine.

SHIFRA
Beautiful. Shifra the midwife, and her colleague Puah, disobeyed Pharaoh's order to kill all male Hebrews at birth. A popular Israeli name.

SHIRA, SHIRI
Song. My song.

SHLOMIT
Peaceful.

SHLOMIYA
Peace.

SHOSHANA
A lily or a rose.

SHULAMIT
Peace. Shula is a nickname.

SIDRA, SIDRAH
Torah portion.

SIMA
Aramaic for gift.

SIMCHA
Joy.

SIMONA, SIMONE
To hear. The feminine of Simon, Simeon.

SIVANA
Ninth month of the year.

SIVIA, SIVYA, TZIVIA
Deer.

T

TAL, TALIA, TALYA, TALI
Dew.

TALMA
Hill.

TAMAR, TAMARA
Date palm. Also, righteous and graceful. A Yiddish variation is Tema.

TEMIMA
Innocent.

TIFERET
Beautiful.

TIKVA
Hope.

TIRA
Castle.

TIRZA
Cypress, also desirable. Tirza was the capital of biblical Samaria.

TORI
My turtledove.

TOVA
Good one. Often Toby in English.

TZAFRIRA
Morning breeze.

TZIPORA
Little bird. Moses' wife. Also spelled Zipporah. Tzipi is a common nickname.

TZURIA
Steadfast.

U

URIT
Light.

V

VARDA
Rose.

VERED
Rose.

VIDA, VITA
Sephardic name meaning life. The equivalent of Eve.

Y

YAEL, YAELA, YAALIT
God is willing. Feminine version of Yoel or Joel.

YAFFA
Beautiful. And the name of an Israeli city.

YAKIRA
Precious.

YARDENA
River Jordan.

YARKONA
Green. Also, the name of both a golden green bird and a river in Israel.

YEDIDA
Friend, beloved. The mother of Josiah, a king of Judah.

YEHIELA
May God live.

YEIRA
Light.

YEMIMA
Dove. A daughter of Job. Jemima in English.

YISRAELA
Israeli or Jew.

YOCHEVED
God is glorious. An unsung matriarch, Yocheved, the wife of Amram, was the mother of Moses, Aaron, and Miriam.

YONA, YONINA, YONIT
Dove.

Z

ZAHARA, ZEHARI
Brightness.

ZAHAVA, ZAHAVI, ZEHAVIT
Golden.

ZARA, ZORA
Variations on Sarah. Also, Zora is Arabic for dawn.

ZEVA
Wolf.

ZIKIT
Longing.

ZILLA, TZILA
Shadow.

ZIONA
Excellent.

ZIVA, ZIVIT
Splendor, radiant.

PART THREE

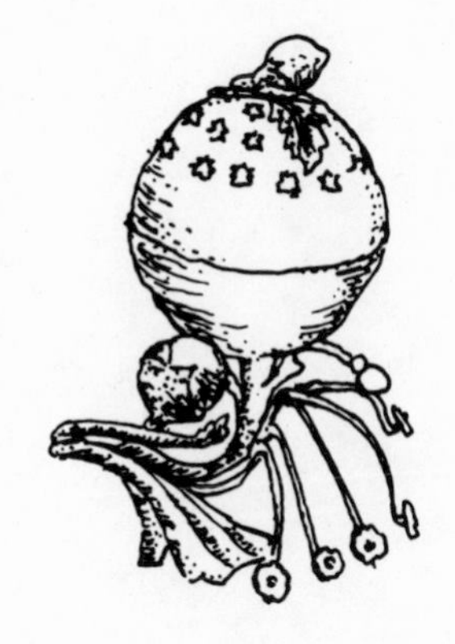

BRIT: COVENANT

COVENANTS

In most ways, *brit milah* and *brit habat* are as different as two ceremonies can be. *Brit milah,* the covenant of circumcision, is the oldest continuous Jewish rite, an act and a ritual that unites Jews throughout ages and across cultures. It is elemental, mysterious, incomprehensible and awe-ful.

Brit habat, on the other hand, while having some basis in Sephardic custom, is a recent invention, an expression of American Judaism in the late twentieth century. It is a rite of passage in the making, and no two *brit habat* ceremonies are quite the same. It is inspiring and often delightful, but because it is so new it is sometimes a little self-conscious.

What *milah* and *habat* have in common is *brit,* covenant. A covenant is a contract—an agreement requiring the assent of the parties involved. The relationship between the people of Israel and God is called covenant; a contract that requires human assent and action.

Many covenants are mentioned in the Torah: Shabbat, the weekly reminder of the creation of the world and of the relationship between God and the Jewish people; the rainbow, a sign of God's universal promise to renew all humankind after the great flood; the Torah itself; and *brit milah,* the covenant of circumcision.

Brit habat is not an imitation of *brit milah;* the two are different, just as male and female are different. But just as Jewish women and Jewish men share in the covenant, so do these two rites of passage.

Bringing a son into the covenant of Israel requires the drawing of blood and setting in the flesh a physical sign of the bond between the Jewish people and God. The absence of a parallel ceremony or mark for daughters has been interpreted in two different ways: as proof that women are second-class citizens not admitted to the covenant; or as a demonstration of women's spiritual superiority for not needing a physical reminder of God's presence.

While some Jews avoid the term *brit habat,* preferring instead terms like *simchat bat* or "baby naming," the convenantal dimension of virtually all new celebrations for daughters is undeniable. Bringing a baby girl before the community—calling her name "in Israel," wishing for "Torah, *huppah* and good deeds" for her future—all this invokes the joys and responsibilities of covenant.

Whether or not you know the sex of your unborn child, read this entire section—both the chapter on *brit milah* and the chapter on *brit habat.* The last section, "*Hiddur Mitzvah:* Beautiful Touches," contains ideas that can be applied to any covenant ceremony—whether you are blessed with a son or a daughter.

BRIT MILAH: THE COVENANT OF CIRCUMCISION

Such shall be the covenant between Me and you and your offspring to follow which you shall keep: every male among you shall be circumcised. You shall circumcise the flesh of your foreskin, and that shall be the sign of the covenant between Me and you.

(Genesis 17:10-11)

It's a boy!

After the initial rush of delight and wonder, comes the realization: we've got to have a *bris!**

The most ancient Jewish rite, a *bris* is traditionally celebrated with feasting and song. It is, above all, a *simcha*—a word that means both joy and its celebration. But many American Jews approach *brit milah* with more confusion and fear than happiness.

This chapter provides you with an overview of the practice and its significance, from theology to the selection of the *mohel,*†

* *The Hebrew word* brit *means covenant, a pledge of obligation usually marked by some kind of token.* Brit milah *is the covenant of circumcision, a physical sign of the unique relationship between the Jewish people and God. Sephardic Jews sometimes refer to the rite simply as* milah. *Since in America the Ashkenazic Hebrew or Yiddish term* bris *is the most familiar name for ritual circumcision, it is used interchangeably with* brit milah.

† *Ritual circumciser. The Yiddish pronunciation is "moil," the Hebrew is "mohail."*

from Torah to physiology. The more you know about the "whys" as well as the "hows" of *brit milah,* the fewer your fears and the greater your rejoicing.

CIRCUMCISION IN HISTORY AND IN THE BIBLE

Circumcision was not unique to the Hebrews. The removal of part or all of the foreskin, the skin covering the glans of the penis, has been practiced by people all over the world. The Egyptians, Phoenicians, and Moabites were among the ancient peoples who circumcised their sons. Usually, circumcision is performed at puberty as part of a rite of initiation into manhood—a proof of courage and fortitude. Among Jews, however, infant circumcision was, and remains, an act of religious consecration and a sign of identity—the first in a lifetime of obligations.

Brit milah is often called the covenant of Abraham because it was first practiced as an expression of faith by the Hebrew patriarch. According to the biblical story, Abram responded to God's command and circumcised himself (according to the *Midrash* at the age of ninety-nine) and all the men of his household, including his thirteen-year-old son Ishmael. In accepting the terms of the covenant, Abram changed his name to Abraham and then followed the practice of naming a son at a circumcision. Isaac, the first son of a circumcised Hebrew, underwent *brit milah* on the eighth day, setting the precedent for the timing of the ritual ever since.

The importance of circumcision as a mark of peoplehood is a constant theme in the Bible. When Moses failed to circumcise his son, his wife Zipporah did it herself in a passage that has excited biblical commentary ever since.[1] And after the forty years in the wilderness, the Hebrews who had suspended the practice during the arduous journey were circumcised before they could enter Canaan.

For every generation, the covenant of circumcision then became a renewed act of commitment to the people of the covenant. And when, during the reign of Queen Jezebel, the Israelites abandoned the covenant of Abraham, the prophet Elijah exhorted the people until they returned to the custom, thereby earning the title "Herald of the Covenant."

Often, circumcision had to be performed in secret, and in many places the sign of the covenant marked Jewish men for execution. The first recorded prohibition against *brit milah* was enacted under Antiochus Epiphanes, the villain in the Book of Maccabees, who executed mothers along with the sons they had circumcised in defiance of his order. Later, one of the causes of the Bar Kochba rebellion was the Roman emperor Hadrian's proscription against *brit milah.*[2]

Over the course of Jewish history, circumcision has been a source of dispute as well as persecution. The Greeks, who worshiped the human body, thought circumcision a desecration. Under Hellenistic rule, many Jews neglected the practice and those who wished to participate in nude Greek games even underwent painful operations to obliterate evidence of the procedure.

During the first century C.E., there was heated debate about whether conversion to Christianity required circumcision, in other words, whether a man had to be a Jew before he could become a Christian. When the opposition to circumcision prevailed, the two faiths split irrevocably. The historical consequences of that decision were sealed when Roman law made it illegal to perform circumcisions for the purpose of conversion to Judaism.

In the nineteenth century, some leaders of the young Reform movement suggested that the custom be abolished. But that position never gained many adherents. Leopold Zunz, a Reform Jew of the era, wrote, "To abrogate circumcision . . . is suicide, not reform."[3]

In the twentieth century, stories from the Holocaust and from the Soviet Union testify to the steadfastness of Jewish practice of *brit milah*—no matter what the consequences. Despite all challenges, it remains a constant feature of the Jewish experience.

TRADITIONAL INTERPRETATIONS

The rabbis who wrote the Talmud and the *Midrash* constructed elaborate overlays of interpretation on every aspect of *brit milah.* The allusions, *midrashim,* and commentaries that relate to *brit milah* could fill a book. What follows is a sampling of those ideas.

The commandment that *brit milah* be performed on the eighth day is explained on many levels. A child who lives for seven full days was thought to gain strength because of contact with his first Shabbat. And while the number seven is associated with the physical world (seven days in the week, seven stages of life), eight is associated with things metaphysical.[4] The eighth day, the addition of one to the natural order, also signifies that *bris* is the culmination of creation, the act that makes a baby *tamim,* perfect or complete, in the sense that Abraham was made *tamim*/perfect in the Torah.

In the Torah, God commands Abram to remove the *orlah,* a word that means not only foreskin but also any barrier standing in the way of a beneficial result. The word *orlah* is also used as a metaphor for obstructions of the heart that prevent a person from hearing or understanding God. Removing the *orlah* is interpreted as a permanent, physical sign of dedication to the ongoing task of perfecting the self in order to be closer to the Holy One.

In the *Midrash,* the story is told that Adam was born without a foreskin, signifying the lack of obstacles between him and God. The foreskin was interpreted as a symbol of Adam's sin—a sign of distance between men and God. Thus, the tradition placed the day of Abraham's circumcision on the tenth of Tishri, the Day of Atonement when sins are forgiven.

The tradition says that Abraham was selected to be the first man marked by circumcision precisely because he saw and heard

God everywhere—because of the lack of barriers between him and the One. *Brit milah* affirms our ability to change not only our habits but our very nature, in order to be closer to God. The rabbis wrote that removing the foreskin was not only a way of sanctifying the act of procreation, but also a means of curbing the powerful sexual drive which might draw men away from God.

The most striking line of the *brit milah* liturgy is, "I saw you wallowing in your blood." The most common interpretation of this passage connects the covenant of *milah* with the covenant of the Hebrew people; the blood is seen as a reference to the physical suffering of the Egyptian captivity. Similarly, the twice-repeated line "because of your blood you shall live" is linked to two signs of Jewish peoplehood: the blood of *milah* and the blood of the Paschal offering.[5]

These lines invite all manner of interpretation. Their insistence on the stuff of the body, and blood in particular (forbidden in so many other contexts), seems to affirm the physical reality of human life, which includes danger, dread, and death as well as spiritual aspirations. Indeed, these earthy, disquieting words are often left untranslated at the ceremony, and in some revised ceremonies, are even replaced with other citations from Torah and Talmud.

MODERN QUESTIONS

Jews have performed the *mitzvah* of *brit milah* in an unbroken chain to this day. Even Jews with little or no connection to community or congregation, even Jews with little or no understanding of the ritual or its meaning, fulfill this most difficult of all the commandments.

Even so, for many American Jews *brit milah* is no longer an automatic response but a decision, a choice made after considering a series of questions. Is it safe? Will my baby suffer? What is the best way to have it done?

Deciding to circumcise a son, especially in the traditional manner, announces your identification with Judaism in a powerful, unequivocal way. Most of all, it challenges you to ask, Why? What does it mean to you? And what do you hope it will mean to him?

Until recently, virtually all Americans circumcised their sons. American physicians used to justify universal circumcision on medical grounds, believing it to be necessary for proper hygiene.[6] As recently as the 1960s, approximately 98 percent of all baby boys born in the United States were circumcised.

But there are few medical arguments in favor of circumcision anymore, a development reflected in figures assembled by the National Center for Health Statistics; in 1985, only 59 percent of newborn boys underwent the procedure. The American Academy of Pediatrics and the American College of Obstetrics and Gynecology state that the routine circumcision of newborn boys is not medically warranted, and the procedure is no longer automatically covered by all medical insurance policies.[7]

This shift in medical opinion coincides with the health consumer movement, which advocates fewer intrusive procedures. The natural childbirth movement reinforces the growing reluctance to subject a newborn to what is commonly called "unnecessary" or even "cosmetic" surgery. Jewish parents attending childbirth preparation classes may find themselves in the uncomfortable position of having to defend a procedure they may find troubling.

For Jews *brit milah* has always been performed as a religious obligation, not as a health measure. But even parents who would never consider *not* circumcising a son have legitimate questions about the procedure.

Am I subjecting my son to physical danger?

Clearly, Jewish sons have survived circumcision for thirty-five hundred years. And a tradition so meticulous about the sanctity of life and health would hardly require an act that might jeopardize either.[8] As far as the health risk is concerned, complications following circumcision are extremely rare. Infection is unlikely in part because the site of the cut is well supplied with blood.[9]

How much will this hurt him?

There can be no definitive answer about the pain the baby suffers. Although some *mohels* and doctors numb the area, *brit milah* is generally performed without anesthesia. Anyone who has attended more than one *bris* can testify that babies are usually easily comforted after the procedure, sucking wine from a finger, nursing, and falling asleep. Some suggest that exposing the baby to cold air and placing him on his back may cause as much discomfort as the cutting itself. There is, however, no minimizing the discomfort that parents feel on their son's behalf.

Mohel or doctor: What is the safest, least traumatic way to have it done?

Some Jews opt for what seems the safer, easier path to satisfying familial pressure to get the baby circumcised by having it done in a hospital by a doctor. There are a number of reasons for this. The stereotype of the *mohel* is that of a doddering old man, while the physician is accorded enormous respect.* If you have a *bris* in the hospital it's done out of sight and earshot.

It is important to remember that a medical circumcision is *not* a *brit milah*. The ritual of *brit milah* includes prayers, expresses the deliberate intent of bringing a son into the covenant, and is performed by a pious Jew. Indeed, a child given a medical circumcision is considered in need of a ritual circumcision called a *hatafat dam brit*, a ritual drawing of blood from the site of the circumcision.

In addition to *halachic* objections to medical circumcision, there are several other factors you might consider when deciding between a hospital "circ" and a *bris* performed by a *mohel* at home. In many cases, inexperienced residents perform the hospital procedure, sometimes doing a few babies one after another. To prevent the baby's moving during the operation, his limbs are strapped onto a board where he may be immobilized for as long as ten or fifteen minutes. Finally, there may not be anyone to hold or comfort the baby afterward.

On the other hand, the *mohel* is an expert at this procedure.

* *There are, in fact,* mohels *who are also physicians.*

(There are many stories about non-Jewish physicians employing *mohels* to circumcise their sons, and it is said that the British royal family entrusts its sons to skilled *mohels.*) If a *mohel* performs a circumcision, you can be certain that yours is the only baby on his mind. In many cases, your son is held by loving human hands during the procedure, and if a safety restraint is used, he will be immobilized for only a few moments.

At a *brit milah,* the baby is given some wine, which is thought to lessen the pain and certainly helps him fall asleep afterward. And when the ceremony is over, he is immediately returned to his mother, who can nurse and comfort him.

Another difference between medical and ritual circumcision concerns timing. Medical circumcisions take place any time between the second and the sixth day, while *brit milah* is never performed before the eighth day. In a full-term baby, substances that regulate blood coagulation and thus facilitate healing are slightly below normal at birth. A further decline in one of these substances occurs between the second and sixth days of life. However, a gradual rise begins after the sixth day, and by the eighth day its presence in the body climbs to above normal levels.[10]

Some parents choose to schedule *brit milah* in the hospital on the eighth day. However, this generally involves readmitting the baby as a patient. This not only exposes the baby to the bacteria present in all hospitals, it also tends to heighten anxiety, and more or less precludes a *simcha.* Who feels like partying in an operating room?

What is the psychological impact of circumcision?

If God had asked Abraham to remove a flap of skin from his elbow and the elbows of all males of his household as a permanent sign of the covenant, *bris* would probably not be the emotionally loaded commandment it is. Then again, had the request not been so difficult, the sign of the covenant might well have been forgotten.

The fact that the mark of the covenant is surgically imprinted on the penis dramatizes the fundamental importance of the act. Certainly, Judaism ascribes enormous significance to circumcision. The Talmud states that "were it not for the blood of the covenant, heaven and earth would not exist." And the philosopher Spinoza declared that the practice of *brit milah* alone would ensure the survival of the Jewish people.

But since Freud, circumcision has been interpreted as symbolic castration. According to the paradigm set forth by the Jewish father of psychoanalysis, male children are potential competitors for their mothers' affections. Sons thus pose a threat to their fathers, which places boys in danger of paternal hostility. From this perspective, circumcision becomes a ritual compromise—a modified castration.

There seems to be little evidence that infants suffer psychosexual damage from the act of circumcision. Whether or not he can localize the pain to his penis, or whether one can properly talk of "memory" in one so young, the baby is certainly not carrying the complex cultural and sexual baggage that causes acute discomfort among his elders. There is little question, however, about the discomfort that *brit milah* causes adults.* It is, after all, an event focused on the penis of a baby, recalling the act that gave him life, and the organ that may one day perpetuate the family as well as the Jewish people.[11]

Brit milah has always been a bittersweet, even ambivalent rite of passage; you voluntarily subject your newborn to pain, and then comfort him as he heals, adding even more heat to the already fevered pitch of parental feelings during the first weeks of life. Although Jewish tradition views *bris* as the occasion for great joy, it also acknowledges the pain it causes parents. Rabbi Shimon bar Yochai said, "Behold, a man loves no one better than his son, and yet he circumcises him!" To which Rabbi Nachman bar Shmuel responded, "He rejoices over the mitzvah even though he sees his son's blood being shed."[12]

Why?

* Brit milah *can be stressful. The baby's older siblings may well respond to the ceremony, celebration and all the attention on the new baby by making difficult demands on everyone. And arguments among the adults are not necessarily the result of sexual anxiety; all rites of passage have a way of bringing family tensions to the surface.*

The apologists who have historically applauded *bris* as a substitute for infant sacrifice or castration inadvertently turn ritual circumcision into the latest stage in the evolution of human sacrifice, a line of thinking that inevitably leads to the question, Why haven't we abandoned so barbaric a practice altogether?

Parents who circumcise their sons do not answer that question with Socratic arguments. The significance and ritual power of *brit milah* is not the stuff of reason or even of language. *Bris* is a radical act of faith, as well as a tangible, physical, visceral connection to our most ancient past. The simplest, most compelling answer to the question of why we do this to our sons is this: If we stop doing *brit milah,* we stop being Jews. And that is a decision that even the most ambivalent among us is loath to make.

LAWS AND CUSTOMS

Brit milah is regulated and elaborated by the laws of the Talmud, with a liturgy that was already old in the first century C.E. *Halachah* clearly spells out the whos, hows, and whens, but the customs associated with *bris* have evolved over time and vary from nation to nation.

The following pages provide a fairly comprehensive guide to *brit milah;* however, no two babies, no two families, no two *brisses* are quite the same. If you have questions about any aspect of the ritual, ask a *mohel* or rabbi. If there are medical issues, consult your pediatrician.

WHEN AND WHERE *Brit milah* takes place on the eighth day of life,* even if it falls on Shabbat or a holiday—including Yom

* *Remember that according to the Jewish calendar, a day begins with the preceding nightfall, so if a boy is born on Monday night, his* bris *would be on the following Tuesday.*

Kippur. Illness or weakness of any kind requires that the rite be postponed until the baby is healthy. However, a *bris* delayed for any reason may not be scheduled on Shabbat or on a holiday, nor can a *bris* for the purpose of conversion, nor on a boy born by cesarean section.

A *bris* may occur anytime before sundown, but it has long been customary to schedule a *bris* early in the day, since the tradition says that one should not delay in performing a *mitzvah*. Early morning is an especially convenient time for a weekday *bris,* so guests may attend before going to work. A light breakfast can then be served as the *s'eudat mitzvah,* the prescribed meal of celebration.

A *bris* may be held anywhere. Although a few hospitals have a special room set aside for ritual circumcisions, today most take place in the home, which is where the ceremony was first performed. From the ninth century and into the twentieth, however, *brit milah* changed from being strictly a family affair to a festival for the whole community, and was commonly observed in the synagogue immediately after morning prayers.[13]

Many traditional communities retain the custom of having a *bris* in the synagogue, with a full meal following. Some liberal congregations now encourage families to use the synagogue for a *bris* as well. In Israel, *brit milah* is often performed and celebrated in catering halls that can accommodate large parties.

WHO The father is responsible for his son's *brit milah,* and technically he performs the circumcision; the *mohel* only acts as his *shaliach* or representative. Even so, the only people who absolutely must be present at a *bris* are the baby, the *mohel* and the *sandek,* who assists by holding the baby.

However, since it is a *mitzvah* to attend a *bris,* tradition considers it a *mitzvah* to inform as many people as possible. You do not "invite" guests to a *bris,* though. Instead, you "announce" it to family and friends.

One of the most welcome guests at every *brit milah* is the prophet Elijah, whose presence is invoked by the *kisei shel Eli-*

yahu, the chair of Elijah. Over the years, the prophet Elijah became a legendary figure: a wanderer, often dressed as a beggar, who came to test the hospitality and worthiness of Jews of all stations in life. There are even tales of saintly rabbis who claimed to see Elijah sitting in his chair during the ritual circumcision.[14]

By the Middle Ages, Elijah's chair was a well-established feature of the *bris.* In many European communities, the synagogue owned an elaborate throne used at all circumcisions. Today, any chair is used—draped, decorated, or adorned with a special pillow.

Among the corporeal guests, parents delegate *kibbudim,* or special honors, to guests who participate in the ritual. Customarily, grandparents are given the most important roles, with other relatives and close friends involved as needed. The most important of these is the *sandek.*

The word is probably derived from the Greek, *syndikos,* meaning patron.[15] The *sandek* assists the *mohel* by holding the baby during the circumcision. In Israel and in more traditional circles, *the sandek* holds the infant on his lap during the *milah*; otherwise he is seated at the table upon which the *bris* is performed.

Given his importance, the *sandek*'s status as a pious Jew was long considered crucial, which is why a community's rabbi was often called upon to hold the baby. In some Sephardic communities, however, the father acts as *sandek* for his own sons.[16] Today in America, grandfathers are often honored with the role.

Traditionally, the *sandek* wears a *tallis,* or prayer shawl, during the ceremony. He is the only one who sits during the ceremony; everyone else stands. In some communities, it is the custom for the *sandek* to pay for the ensuing feast.

In addition to the *sandek* there are other ceremonial roles that may be distributed to family and friends. Eastern European Jews developed the role and title of *kvatterin* (godmother), who carries the baby from the mother to the room where the *bris* takes place, and the *kvatter* (godfather), who in turn brings the baby to the chair of Elijah.

This kind of honor can be tailored to include more or fewer guests, depending upon the configuration of family and friends. For example, if you are fortunate enough to have both grandfathers present, the two men can share the honors of *sandek,* with one holding the baby during the circumcision and the other doing the honors during the naming. If a rabbi or cantor is present, he or she might be asked to read or chant the naming blessings.

In general, it is a *mitzvah* to include as many people as possible in the ceremony. Other honors might include designating someone to carry the baby back to his mother, or having four friends hold a prayer shawl over the *bris,* recalling the parents' wedding canopy. In some communities, it was customary to designate some honors to a couple trying to conceive, to invoke the luck and blessings of the new parents on them.

On the other hand, it's perfectly fine to keep things simple. Remember, the law only requires the active participation of *sandek* and *mohel.* If you like, you can involve more people at the celebration afterward. The section Simcha Means Party talks more about this.

In the past, women had no active role in *brit milah;* indeed they were not even in attendance. In some Orthodox communities, this is still the case. Among Orthodox Ashkenazic Jews, the *kibbudim* for women were limited to handing the baby from one generation to the next, from aunt to cousin to sister. Liberal Jews, however, have expanded women's roles to include virtually all the traditional honors, although the role of *sandek* tends to be reserved for a male relative.

There is a wide range of modern custom regarding the mother's participation. Some choose to remain out of sight and out of earshot during their son's circumcision, while some mothers join in reciting the blessing, believing that the responsibility of *brit milah* is shared by both parents. Other mothers carry the baby into the room, witness the circumcision, and add a prayer or give a *d'var torah* afterward.

Full participation by mothers, while not specifically forbidden by tradition, is problematic for some *mohels.* While one *mohel* may object to a woman reciting the blessing required of the father, another may encourage the mother's full participation. If you have strong feelings about having both parents share in the rituals of *brit milah,* you should discuss this during preliminary conversations with *mohels.*

Women's participation in ritual life has widened across the spectrum of Jewish observance. Even in very traditional communities, there is one prayer mothers often recite—*birkat hagomel,* the blessing of thanks after recovery from childbirth or any other life-threatening situation.

This blessing is spoken in the presence of a *minyan* and can be part of *brit milah.*

The mother says:

בָּרוּךְ אַתָּה יְיָ, אֱלֹהֵינוּ מֶלֶךְ הָעוֹלָם, הַגּוֹמֵל לְחַיָּבִים טוֹבוֹת, שֶׁגְּמָלַנִי כָּל טוֹב.

Blessed are You, Adonai, Ruler of All, who does good to the undeserving and who has dealt kindly with me.

The community responds:

מִי שֶׁגְּמָלְךָ כָּל טוֹב, הוּא יִגְמָלְךָ כָּל טוֹב, סֶלָה.

May the One who has shown you kindness deal kindly with you forever.

Sephardic and Mizrachi (Middle Eastern) customs offer interesting models for women's participation. In some families, it is traditional for the mother, flanked by both grandmothers, to bring the baby to the *sandek.* While the guests sing, the women approach Elijah's chair three times and withdraw three times in a kind of ritual dance. Elsewhere, the mother makes her appearance in a long white dress at the *s'eudat mitzvah,* where she is given some wine from the cup blessed by the *mohel* during the ceremony.[17]

THE MOHEL *Mohels* are not ordained like rabbis, yet their status as important Jewish functionaries has been acknowledged since at least the first century C.E.[18] Traditionally, one becomes a *mohel* by apprenticeship, through study with and supervision by an accomplished, established *mohel,* someone versed in the *halachah* as well as the techniques of *milah.* But, in fact, anyone can hang out a shingle and proclaim himself* a *mohel.* There is virtually no regulation or registration for *mohels* in America as there is in Great Britain.[19] Word of mouth recommendation is really the only form of control or regulation.

There are few full-time *mohels.* Most perform ritual circumcisions "on the side," as both a *mitzvah* and an additional source of income. Many American *mohels* are also rabbis or cantors and there is a growing number of *mohel*-physicians.

For a number of years, there has been a *mohel* shortage in much of the United States, especially in smaller communities, a fact that has contributed to the increase in hospital circumcisions among Jews. To respond to this need, and also to expedite the Reform movement's acceptance of children born to Jewish fathers and non-Jewish mothers, the Reform Union of American Hebrew Congregations certifies physicians already performing medical circumcisions as Reform *mohels.*† The UAHC training, for board-certified doctors only, consists of a course of study about the theology, *halachah,* folklore, and liturgy of *brit milah.*

The certification of Reform *mohels* is nearly as controversial as the policy of patrilineal descent, and some traditional Jews do not recognize these physicians as *mohels.* Nevertheless, Jewish law permits *brit milah* to be performed by virtually any Jew,

* *While the Reform movement has certified some female physicians as* mohels, *the role is traditionally and still overwhelmingly held by men; thus, all references to* mohels *are masculine.*

† *The Conservative movement is considering a similar program.*

though the tradition is firm in its preference for pious male Jews.[20]

Although the honors may be shared with a rabbi, the *mohel* generally acts as the *mesader habrit,* the one who orders the *bris.* As master of ceremonies, he sets the tone of the event. He can put everyone at ease, calm anxiety, and foster a spirit of *simcha.* To ensure that everyone present understands the profound importance and joyfulness of *brit milah,* many *mohels* include some teaching about its history and religious significance.

A *mohel's* style can be abrupt and businesslike, gently spiritual, musically inspiring, Borscht-belt shtick, or any combination of the above. Clearly, the choice of a *mohel,* like that of a rabbi for a wedding, is important on many levels.

Often, there is no question of choosing a *mohel* since many communities have only one or two practitioners of the ancient art. But where there is some selection, most people select a *mohel* on the recommendation of people they trust. Since rabbis and cantors go to a lot of *brisses,* they are good people to consult.

Few cities have a registry of *mohels,* but the offices of your local Orthodox, Conservative, and Reform rabbinic organizations may be able to provide you with a list. Some *mohels* even place advertisements in Jewish newspapers. If you contact one through such an ad, he should provide you with references.

Your first contact with the *mohel* will be over the telephone. In the not-so-distant past parents would only call after the baby was born. While this is still standard operating procedure, it is increasingly common for parents to call much earlier in the pregnancy, whether or not prenatal tests indicate a male child.

A prebirth call should, first of all, ascertain whether he will be available around the due date. (Even *mohels* take vacations.) Also, ask about the fee. Most charge a flat rate for the ceremony, adding travel expenses if there is any distance involved. If you cannot afford the fee, let the *mohel* know; most are willing to reduce their fees if there is a problem.

Once the baby arrives, a phone call can establish the hour for the ritual, and the *mohel* will give you instructions about the items he requires (such as cloth diapers, kosher wine and a goblet for *kiddush,* prayer shawls, a table, chairs, cotton balls, gauze pads, petroleum jelly, and so forth). If at all possible, this is done at a pre-*bris* meeting, when the *mohel* can also examine the baby. He may well ask about the parents' and the baby's Hebrew names. Do not leave the decision of your son's Hebrew name to the morning of the *bris;* if you need advice, ask the *mohel* or your rabbi well before the big day.

The *mohel* might also pose some more difficult questions. It may seem cruel for someone to raise the volatile issue of "Who is a Jew?" at this moment in your lives; however, the *mohel* has obligations beyond providing you with a service. Because he has a responsibility to Jewish tradition as he interprets it, the *mohel* has to ascertain whether he can perform your son's *bris.* Thus, some observant *mohels* will not perform a *bris* on, say, a baby born of a mother who was converted by a Reform rabbi.

Interpretation of law varies from one person to the next, but it is disrespectful and pointless to insist on something one man cannot, in conscience, do. You can avoid a lot of grief by doing some homework about local *mohels,* and speaking with them in advance of the baby's birth.

On the day of your son's *brit milah,* the *mohel* will examine the baby before the ceremony begins. If there are any questions about the baby's health, Jewish law obliges him to postpone the *bris.* Once he is satisfied that your son is all right, the *mohel* will probably want to talk to the *sandek,* and confer with you about other guests who will be honored during the ceremony.

After the circumcision, the *mohel* may or may not stay for the *s'eudat mitzvah,* depending on his schedule. However, before leaving, he should examine the baby and give you complete instructions about taking care of the circumcision. (See below.) In the days when *mohels* served small, compact communities, they generally made house calls within a few days of the *bris* to change the dressing and check on the baby's progress. Given modern geographical realities, follow-up is commonly done by telephone.

You should feel free to call the *mohel* at any time with questions about your son's healing.

THE CEREMONY

The liturgy of *brit milah* was fixed by the first century. As with most Jewish life-cycle rituals, the ceremony is very brief—no more than five minutes long.

A *bris* consists of three parts—the first is as normative and universal as any part of Jewish religious life: A blessing is made, the circumcision is performed, and another blessing follows.

The second part begins with *kiddush,* the blessing over wine, and includes a longer chanted prayer that gives the baby his name; this section is the most amenable to additions and changes.

The third requirement is the *s'eudat mitzvah,* the ritual meal of celebration, which is described further in the chapter "Simcha Means Party."

The core of a traditional *brit milah* ceremony follows.

SEDER HABRIT MILAH
The Order of the Covenant of Circumcision

As the infant is carried in, everyone greets him with the phrase:

בָּרוּךְ הַבָּא

Baruch haba.

Blessed is the one who comes.

After the baby is brought into the room, he is placed on Elijah's chair, and then handed to the *sandek.* Just before performing the circumcision, the *mohel* recites:

בָּרוּךְ אַתָּה יְיָ, אֱלֹהֵינוּ מֶלֶךְ הָעוֹלָם אֲשֶׁר קִדְּשָׁנוּ בְּמִצְוֹתָיו, וְצִוָּנוּ עַל הַמִּילָה.

Blessed are You, Adonai our God, Ruler of the Universe, Who sanctifies us with commandments and commands us regarding circumcision.

He removes the foreskin, making sure that there is at least one drop of blood visible. As soon as this is accomplished, the father recites, or repeats after the *mohel*:

בָּרוּךְ אַתָּה יְיָ, אֱלֹהֵינוּ מֶלֶךְ הָעוֹלָם אֲשֶׁר קִדְּשָׁנוּ בְּמִצְוֹתָיו, וְצִוָּנוּ לְהַכְנִיסוֹ בִּבְרִיתוֹ שֶׁל אַבְרָהָם אָבִינוּ.

Baruch ata Adonai Eloheinu melech ha'olam asher kidshanu b'miztvotav v'tzivanu l'hachniso bivrito shel Avraham aveinu.

Blessed are You, Adonai our God, Ruler of the universe, Who sanctifies us with Your commandments and commands us to bring our son into the convenant of Abraham, our father.

Everyone present then answers with an Amen, and responds:

כְּשֵׁם שֶׁנִּכְנַס לַבְּרִית, כֵּן יִכָּנֵס לְתוֹרָה וּלְחֻפָּה וּלְמַעֲשִׂים טוֹבִים.

K'shem she'nich-nas la-brit, ken yi-ka-nes l'Torah, u'le'chup-pah u'le'maasim tovim.

Just as he entered the covenant, so may he enter into the world of Torah, the wedding canopy and the accomplishment of good deeds.

Meanwhile, the *mohel* attends to the baby. He recites *kiddush,* drinks from the cup, and gives some to the baby.

בָּרוּךְ אַתָּה יְיָ, אֱלֹהֵינוּ מֶלֶךְ הָעוֹלָם, בּוֹרֵא פְּרִי הַגָּפֶן.

Baruch ata Adonai Eloheinu melech ha'olam, borei p'ri ha-gafen.

Blessed are You, Adonai our God, Ruler of the Universe, who creates the fruit of the vine.

The following blessings follow immediately and may be recited by the *mohel* or another honored guest, often a rabbi.

בָּרוּךְ אַתָּה יְיָ, אֱלֹהֵינוּ מֶלֶךְ הָעוֹלָם אֲשֶׁר קִדֵּשׁ יְדִיד מִבֶּטֶן, וְחֹק בִּשְׁאֵרוֹ שָׂם, וְצֶאֱצָאָיו חָתַם בְּאוֹת בְּרִית קֹדֶשׁ. עַל כֵּן, בִּשְׂכַר זֹאת, אֵל חַי, חֶלְקֵנוּ צוּרֵנוּ, צַוֵּה לְהַצִּיל יְדִידוּת שְׁאֵרֵנוּ מִשַּׁחַת, לְמַעַן בְּרִיתוֹ אֲשֶׁר שָׂם בִּבְשָׂרֵנוּ. בָּרוּךְ אַתָּה יְיָ, כּוֹרֵת הַבְּרִית.

Blessed are You, God, Source of Life, Who sanctifies your beloved from birth and who has impressed Your decree in his flesh, and marked this offspring with the sign of the holy covenant. Therefore, for the sake of this covenant, oh Living God, our Portion, our Rock, protect this child from all misfortune, for the sake of Your covenant that You have placed in our flesh. Blessed are You, Adonai, Who establishes the covenant.

אֱלֹהֵינוּ וֵאלֹהֵי אֲבוֹתֵינוּ, קַיֵּם אֶת הַיֶּלֶד הַזֶּה לְאָבִיו וּלְאִמּוֹ, וְיִקָּרֵא שְׁמוֹ, בְּיִשְׂרָאֵל ________ בֶּן ________. יִשְׂמַח הָאָב בְּיוֹצֵא חֲלָצָיו, וְתָגֵל אִמּוֹ בִּפְרִי בִטְנָהּ. כַּכָּתוּב: יִשְׂמַח אָבִיךָ וְאִמֶּךָ, וְתָגֵל יוֹלַדְתֶּךָ.[1] וְנֶאֱמַר: וָאֶעֱבֹר עָלַיִךְ וָאֶרְאֵךְ מִתְבּוֹסֶסֶת בְּדָמָיִךְ, וָאֹמַר לָךְ בְּדָמַיִךְ חֲיִי, וָאֹמַר לָךְ בְּדָמַיִךְ חֲיִי.[2] וְנֶאֱמַר: זָכַר לְעוֹלָם בְּרִיתוֹ, דָּבָר צִוָּה לְאֶלֶף דּוֹר. אֲשֶׁר כָּרַת אֶת אַבְרָהָם, וּשְׁבוּעָתוֹ לְיִצְחָק. וַיַּעֲמִידֶהָ לְיַעֲקֹב לְחֹק, לְיִשְׂרָאֵל בְּרִית עוֹלָם.[3] וְנֶאֱמַר. וַיָּמָל אַבְרָהָם אֶת יִצְחָק בְּנוֹ, בֶּן שְׁמֹנַת יָמִים, כַּאֲשֶׁר צִוָּה אֹתוֹ אֱלֹהִים.[4] הוֹדוּ לַייָ כִּי טוֹב, כִּי לְעוֹלָם חַסְדּוֹ. הוֹדוּ לַיהוה כִּי טוֹב, כִּי טוֹב, כִּי לְעוֹלָם חַסְדּוֹ.[5] זֶה הַקָּטָן גָּדוֹל יִהְיֶה. כְּשֵׁם שֶׁנִּכְנַס לַבְּרִית, כֵּן יִכָּנֵס לְתוֹרָה, וּלְחֻפָּה, וּלְמַעֲשִׂים טוֹבִים.

Our God and God of our ancestors, sustain this child for his father and mother, and may he be called ________________, son of ________________.

May his father rejoice in the issue of his loins and may his mother exult in the fruit of her womb, as it is written, "Your father and mother will rejoice. She who bore you will exult."

And it is said, When I passed by you and saw you wallowing

in your blood I said to you, "Because of your blood you shall live!" and I said to you, "Because of your blood you shall live!"

And it is said, "God is ever mindful of God's covenant, the promise given for a thousand generations. That which God made with Abraham, swore to Isaac, and confirmed in a decree for Jacob, for Israel as an eternal covenant."

And it is said, "When his son Isaac was eight days old, Abraham circumcised him, as God had commanded him."

Praise God for God is good. God's steadfast love is forever.

May this child, ________________, grow into manhood. As he has entered the covenant, so may he enter the study of Torah, the wedding canopy and the accomplishment of good deeds.

The *mohel* will usually offer another prayer for the well-being of the baby, and another asking God to accept his work. Other prayers may be added at this point. Sephardic Jews recite *kaddish,* marking the arrival of a new Jewish soul to replenish the loss of those commemorated by this prayer.[21]

The familiar words and melody of the *shehehiyanu,* the prayer of thanksgiving, is often included as well. In Israel, it follows upon the father's blessing immediately after the circumcision.[22]

There are countless traditional variations and customs attached to this simple ceremony. The father may hand the *izmail,* the circumcision knife, to the *mohel,* demonstrating that he bears responsibility for the act. And Sephardic Jews follow the blessing over wine by enjoying the scent of fragrant spices—Moroccan Jews use dried rose petals—and recite the blessing over spices familiar from *havdalah.*

בָּרוּךְ אַתָּה יְיָ, אֱלֹהֵינוּ מֶלֶךְ הָעוֹלָם, בּוֹרֵא מִינֵי בְשָׂמִים.

Blessed are You, Source of Life, who makes fragrant spices.

Finally, the ritual ends and the *s'eudat mitzvah* begins with the singing of *Siman Tov Umazel Tov,* a universal song of rejoicing.

NEW CUSTOMS

Recently, parents have been recovering customs of *brit milah* that fell out of use in the past few generations in America, as well as incorporating a few innovations. Generally, additions to the ceremony tend to be simple and brief, the business of *milah* and the comfort of the baby being paramount.

There is renewed interest in *kibbudim,* or honors, for family members and friends. Sometimes, the baby is passed from one generation to the next, from the grandparents (or, if you are so blessed, great-grandparents) to the parents. If an older sibling is mature enough to participate, he or she might carry the baby into the room, or light a candle, or even offer a blessing.

After the circumcision, it is now customary for one or both parents to say a few words about the baby's name. If he is being named for a relative who has died, it can be a very moving moment in remembrance of a loved one and to voice hopes that your new son will grow up to be like him.

At this point, guests might also be asked to offer blessings for the new baby: May he be blessed with long life; May he grow up in a world free of want and fear; May he know the happiness of his family's love forever; May he inherit his mother's good looks and his father's appetite. If this idea appeals to you, you can ask your guests to give it some thought in advance. Wishes like these can be recorded in a very special kind of guest book.

Some parents provide a printed guide that explains the history and meaning of *brit milah,* or provides responsive readings for the ceremony. This pamphlet traditionally lists the prayers recited after meals, including special blessings for the *s'eudat* that follows a *bris.* (See the chapter on *Simcha* for more on booklets.)

Probably the most radical departure from tradition is the custom of having the *milah* take place privately, with only the immediate family present. A "naming" then takes place a few weeks later in the context of a larger celebration and *s'eudat mitzvah.* This separation of the two parts of the ceremony is sometimes done because the mother cannot attend a *bris* eight days after the birth due to ill health. But in some cases, the family feels strongly that their baby's pain should not coincide with a party. There is some precedent for this notion, since Abraham's celebration of Isaac's birth took place at his weaning and not at his circumcision.

In the same spirit, some parents have the circumcision performed in a small room away from most of the guests. In the meanwhile, or shortly thereafter, the other guests are involved in the naming blessings.

Parents who choose hospital circumcision sometimes request that a naming ceremony for their son be held later in the synagogue. Responses to this request vary from rabbi to rabbi. The most traditional will insist upon a *hatafat dam brit,* a ritual drawing of blood from the site of the circumcision, which fulfills the obligations of *brit milah,* before reciting the naming blessing. Some rabbis regularly officiate at such namings. Still others apply the Talmudic category of *LaHatchilah Lo, DeAvad Een,* which means, "If you ask me before you do it, I'll say no; if you tell me after the fact, I'll say, well, all right," but participate only at a private ceremony that cannot encourage other members of their congregations to follow suit.[23]

BRIT MILAH FOR CONVERSION

An adopted infant son is circumcised in a *brit milah* as soon as possible. If the baby was not born to a Jewish mother, a *bet din,* a court of three pious Jews, attends a *bris* for the purpose of conversion. The ritual is the same except for the *mohel's* blessings before performing the *milah*:

בָּרוּךְ אַתָּה יְיָ, אֱלֹהֵינוּ מֶלֶךְ הָעוֹלָם אֲשֶׁר קִדְּשָׁנוּ בְּמִצְוֹתָיו, וְצִוָּנוּ לָמוּל אֶת־הַגֵּרִים.

Holy One of Blessing, Your Presence fills creation, You make us holy with Your commandments, calling us to circumcise the convert.

בָּרוּךְ אַתָּה יְיָ, אֱלֹהֵינוּ מֶלֶךְ הָעוֹלָם אֲשֶׁר קִדְּשָׁנוּ בְּמִצְוֹתָיו, וְצִוָּנוּ לָמוּל אֶת־הַגֵּרִים וּלְהַטִּיף מֵהֶם דַּם בְּרִית שֶׁאִלְמָלֵא דַּם בְּרִית לֹא נִתְקַיְּמוּ שָׁמַיִם וָאָרֶץ, שֶׁנֶּאֱמַר: אִם־לֹא בְרִיתִי יוֹמָם וָלָיְלָה חֻקּוֹת שָׁמַיִם וָאָרֶץ לֹא־שָׂמְתִּי. בָּרוּךְ אַתָּה יְיָ, כּוֹרֵת הַבְּרִית.

Holy One of Blessing, Your Presence fills creation, You make us holy with Your commandments, calling us to circumcise the convert, and to draw the blood of the convert. Were it not for the blood of the covenant, heaven and earth would not have been fulfilled, as it is said, without My covenant, I would not set forth day and night and the laws of heaven and earth. Holy One of Blessing, author of the covenant.

To acknowledge the special dimension of the *brit milah* for an adopted son, the following prayer might be added:

Parents:
We are grateful to God
Who has made this miracle of creation
And given us this baby boy.
His coming into our home has blessed us.
He is part of our family and our lives.
This child has now become our son.

Out of our love of God and Torah and Israel,
We wish to raise him up as a Jew.
We come now before a Jewish court of three
To begin his entry into the Jewish people
Through the mitzvah of milah.
Let this be the beginning
Of his living a life of mitzvot.

May we be privileged to raise him up
As a true and loyal son of Abraham and Sarah.

One of the Court:
This child comes into the covenant in our presence.

We welcome him with the words that God spoke to Abraham our father:
"Hit-halech l'fanai veh-yeh tamim;
Walk before Me and be whole."[24]

Once your son has healed, he is taken to *mikvah* where, in the presence of a rabbinical court of three, the child is immersed in the ritual bath. Some say this should be done as soon as possible, while others suggest waiting till the baby is three years old. The blessing for *mikvah* and a *shehehiyanu* are then recited. In some circles, the Hebrew name is given during *brit milah*; in others, it is not given or announced until after *mikvah*. (See the chapter on Adoption for a full discussion of laws and customs as well as ceremonies.)

According to *halachah,* the son of a Jewish father and a non-Jewish mother must be converted—given a *brit milah,* with the amended blessing by the *mohel,* and then immersed in a *mikvah* —before he is considered a Jew. However, the children of a woman who has converted to Judaism are considered Jews, and there is no difference between the son of a born Jew and a Jew-by-choice. However, Orthodox Jews and the state of Israel do not recognize conversions performed by Reform, Reconstructionist or Conservative rabbis. Thus someday, in certain quarters, there may be a question as to the Jewishness of children born to a mother whose conversion was not supervised by Orthodox rabbis. Families with concerns about this matter should discuss them with their rabbi.

RITUAL CIRCUMCISION

If an adopted non-Jewish child has already been circumcised, a *hatafat dam brit* is performed as soon as possible. This ritual involves drawing a drop of blood from the site of the circumcision. Although a *mohel* should draw the blood, no blessings are required. However, since this is a covenantal moment, *shehehiyanu, kiddush,* and other blessings and prayers are very appropriate. Technically, a *hatafat dam brit* does not require a *s'eudat mitzvah,* but that is no reason to forgo a celebration of such a happy event.

Since this rite involves virtually no wound or healing, *hatafat dam brit* is often held at the *mikvah,* where the immersion follows, witnessed by a *bet din.* The baby may be named at the *mikvah* or you may want to postpone the naming until it can be held in the presence of a joyous company and followed by a festive meal. (Again, see the chapter on Adoption.)

Hatafat dam brit is also performed on children born to Jewish mothers but who were circumcised without Jewish ritual. Again, the *mohel* will officiate, and although no blessings are required, you may want to create a ceremony of celebration that includes traditional elements.

CARING FOR THE NEWLY CIRCUMCISED BABY

Your *mohel* should provide you with information about the care of the circumcision. This advice will vary from practitioner to practitioner.

Many *mohels* will apply a vaseline-saturated gauze bandage that will fall off in two to four days. During those first few days, you might see pink stains on the baby's diapers. This is almost always coagulated blood dissolved by urination, and is not a cause for alarm. Once the bandages come off, the penis will be bright red at first, but the redness will subside within a few weeks at most. A lymphatic secretion may appear on the shaft of the penis; just leave it alone and it too will go away.

Your *mohel* may give you specific instructions about applying an antibacterial salve or ointment, but generally, the less you do, the better. By your first visit to the pediatrician—within your baby's first month—it should be completely healed.

If at any time you have any concerns or questions about how your son is doing, call the *mohel*—or your pediatrician.

NEW LITURGIES

The *brit milah* ceremony above does not include the variations, songs, and chanted verses that add so much to the ritual. The rabbi's manuals for the movements of American Judaism each include a service for *brit milah* with suggested readings for the rabbi, for parents, grandparents, and for the assembled company. Your own rabbi, and/or *mohel,* will doubtless have a service to suggest.

Most parents are happy just to follow the *mohel*'s and/or rabbi's directions. The power of the ancient ceremony and the anxiety associated with circumcision explain the relative absence of liturgical innovation for *brit milah.* The following two ceremonies do not stray very far from traditional *brit milah.* However, they do include innovations in Hebrew as well as English, traditional and nontraditional prayers.

COVENANT OF CIRCUMCISION[25]
for Jacob Nathan

Jacob is brought in and everyone says:

בָּרוּךְ הַבָּא

Baruch haba.

Blessed be he who enters.

The parents say:

הִנְנִי מוּכָן/נָה וּמְזֻמָּן/מְזֻמֶּנָה מֶנֶת לְקַיֵּם מִצְוַת עֲשֵׂה, שֶׁצִּוָּנוּ הַבּוֹרֵא יִתְבָּרֵךְ,
לָמוּל אֶת בְּנִי כַּכָּתוּב בַּתּוֹרָה: „וּבֶן־שְׁמֹנַת יָמִים יִמּוֹל לָכֶם כָּל זָכָר לְדֹרֹתֵיכֶם.״

We are ready to fulfill the precept of circumcising our son, as the blessed Creator has commanded us. As it is written in the Torah: "And throughout the generations, every male among you shall be circumcised at the age of eight days."

Jacob is placed on the *sandek*'s lap. The *mohel* says:

זֶה הַכִּסֵּא שֶׁל אֵלִיָּהוּ זָכוּר לַטּוֹב.
לִישׁוּעָתְךָ קִוִּיתִי יְיָ. שִׂבַּרְתִּי לִישׁוּעָתְךָ, יְיָ, וּמִצְוֹתֶיךָ עָשִׂיתִי. שִׂבַּרְתִּי לִישׁוּעָתְךָ, יְיָ. שָׂשׂ אָנֹכִי עַל אִמְרָתֶךָ, כְּמוֹצֵא שָׁלָל רָב. שָׁלוֹם רָב לְאֹהֲבֵי תוֹרָתֶךָ, וְאֵין לָהֶם מִכְשׁוֹל. אַשְׁרֵי תִּבְחַר וּתְקָרֵב, יִשְׁכֹּן חֲצֵרֶיךָ.

This is the chair of Elijah of blessed memory. God, I hope for your saving power. I await your deliverance, O God, and I follow your commandments. I delight in each of your words, finding great riches in them. May those who love Your Torah have abundant peace, may there be no obstacle before them. Happy is the one You choose and bring near to dwell in your courts.

All recite:

נִשְׂבְּעָה בְּטוּב בֵּיתֶךָ, קְדוֹשׁ הֵיכָלֶךָ.

May we fully enjoy the goodness of Your house, Your holy temple.

The *mohel* says:

בָּרוּךְ אַתָּה יְיָ, אֱלֹהֵינוּ מֶלֶךְ הָעוֹלָם אֲשֶׁר קִדְּשָׁנוּ בְּמִצְוֹתָיו, וְצִוָּנוּ עַל הַמִּילָה.

Blessed are You, God, Ruler of the universe, who has made us holy with your commandments and commanded us to perform circumcision.

The circumcision is performed. The parents say:

בָּרוּךְ אַתָּה יְיָ, אֱלֹהֵינוּ מֶלֶךְ הָעוֹלָם אֲשֶׁר קִדְּשָׁנוּ בְּמִצְוֹתָיו, וְצִוָּנוּ לְהַכְנִיסוֹ בִּבְרִיתוֹ שֶׁל אַבְרָהָם אָבִינוּ.

Blessed are You, God, Ruler of the universe, who has made us holy with Your commandments and commanded us to bring our son into the covenant of Abraham our father.

Parents recite *shehehiyanu* and the guests say:

כְּשֵׁם שֶׁנִּכְנַס לַבְּרִית, כֵּן יִכָּנֵס לְתוֹרָה וּלְחֻפָּה וּלְמַעֲשִׂים טוֹבִים.

As he has entered the covenant, so may he enter the study of Torah, the wedding canopy and the accomplishment of good deeds.

The blessing over wine is said and Jacob is given a few drops. The *mohel* says:

בָּרוּךְ אַתָּה יְיָ, אֱלֹהֵינוּ מֶלֶךְ הָעוֹלָם, אֲשֶׁר קִדֵּשׁ יְדִיד מִבֶּטֶן, וְחֹק בִּשְׁאֵרוֹ שָׂם, וְצֶאֱצָאִים חָתַם בְּאוֹת בְּרִית קֹדֶשׁ. עַל כֵּן, בִּשְׂכַר זֹאת, אֵל חַי, צַוֵּה לְהַצִּיל יְדִידוּת שְׁאֵרֵנוּ מִשַּׁחַת, לְמַעַן בְּרִיתוֹ אֲשֶׁר שָׂם בִּבְשָׂרֵנוּ. בָּרוּךְ אַתָּה יְיָ, כּוֹרֵת הַבְּרִית.

Blessed are You, God, Source of Life, who has sanctified your beloved from birth, who has impressed Your statute upon the flesh and the heart, and who has marked the offspring with the sign of the holy covenant. Therefore, for the sake of this covenant, O living God, our Portion, our Rock, protect this child from all misfortune, for the sake of the covenant which you have set in our flesh and in our hearts. Blessed are You, God, Maker of the covenant.

אֱלֹהֵינוּ וֵאלֹהֵי אֲבוֹתֵינוּ וְאִמּוֹתֵינוּ, קַיֵּם אֶת הַיֶּלֶד הַזֶּה לְאָבִיו וּלְאִמּוֹ, וְיִקָּרֵא שְׁמוֹ בְּיִשְׂרָאֵל יַעֲקֹב נָתָן עֵץ־חַיִּים בֶּן שְׁמוּאֵל נָתָן עֵץ־חַיִּים וַאֲבִיבָה צְבִיָּה.

Our God and God of our fathers and mothers, sustain this child for his father and mother, and may he be called Jacob Nathan, son of Samuel and Aviva.

Parents say:

יִשְׂמַח הָאָב בְּיוֹצֵא חֲלָצָיו, וְתָגֵל אִמּוֹ בִּפְרִי בִטְנָהּ, כַּכָּתוּב: יִשְׂמַח אָבִיךָ וְאִמֶּךָ וְתָגֵל יוֹלַדְתֶּךָ.

May the father and mother rejoice in their offspring, as it is written, "Your father and mother will rejoice. She who bore you will exult."

The company reads the following verses in Hebrew and English:

וְנֶאֱמַר: וָאֶעֱבֹר עָלַיִךְ וָאֶרְאֵךְ מִתְבּוֹסֶסֶת בְּדָמָיִךְ, וָאֹמַר לָךְ בְּדָמַיִךְ חֲיִי: וָאֹמַר לָךְ בְּדָמַיִךְ חֲיִי. . . . וָאֶפְרֹשׂ כְּנָפִי עָלַיִךְ וָאֲכַסֶּה עֶרְוָתֵךְ וָאֶשָּׁבַע לָךְ וָאָבוֹא בִבְרִית אֹתָךְ נְאֻם אֲדֹנָי יֱהוִה וַתִּהְיִי־לִי.

And it is said: "When I passed by you and saw you wallowing in your blood I said to you: 'Live in spite of your blood.' I said to you, 'Live in spite of your blood.' . . . I spread my robe over you and covered your nakedness, and I entered into a covenant with you by oath—declared God; thus you became Mine."

וְנֶאֱמַר: זָכַר לְעוֹלָם בְּרִיתוֹ, דָּבָר צִוָּה לְאֶלֶף דּוֹר. אֲשֶׁר כָּרַת אֶת אַבְרָהָם, וּשְׁבוּעָתוֹ לְיִצְחָק. וַיַּעֲמִידֶהָ לְיַעֲקֹב לְחֹק, לְיִשְׂרָאֵל בְּרִית עוֹלָם.

And it is said, "God is ever mindful of God's covenant, the promise given for a thousand generations. That which God made with Abraham, swore to Isaac, and confirmed in a decree for Jacob, for Israel as an eternal covenant."

וְנֶאֱמַר: וַיָּמָל אַבְרָהָם אֶת יִצְחָק בְּנוֹ בֶּן־שְׁמֹנַת יָמִים, כַּאֲשֶׁר צִוָּה אֹתוֹ אֱלֹהִים.

And it is said, "And when Isaac was eight days old, Abraham circumcised him, as God had commanded him."

הוֹדוּ לַיְיָ כִּי טוֹב, כִּי לְעוֹלָם חַסְדּוֹ.

Praise God for God is good, God's steadfast love is forever.

וּמָל יְהוָה אֱלֹהֶיךָ אֶת־לְבָבְךָ וְאֶת לְבַב זַרְעֶךָ, לְאַהֲבָה אֶת־יְהוָה אֱלֹהֶיךָ בְּכָל־לְבָבְךָ וּבְכָל נַפְשְׁךָ לְמַעַן חַיֶּיךָ.

Then God will circumcise your heart and the hearts of your offspring to love God with all your heart and soul, in order that you may live.

The *mohel* says:

זֶה הַקָּטָן יַעֲקֹב נָתָן גָּדוֹל יִהְיֶה. כְּשֵׁם שֶׁנִּכְנַס לַבְּרִית, כֵּן יִכָּנֵס לְתוֹרָה וּלְחֻפָּה וּלְמַעֲשִׂים טוֹבִים.

May this child Jacob Nathan grow into manhood. As he has entered the covenant, so may he enter the study of Torah, the wedding canopy, and the accomplishment of good deeds.

The parents tell their guests about the baby's names. Then, Jacob is passed from person to person, so each may greet and welcome him; meanwhile, everyone hums *niggunim,* wordless melodies, that have special meaning to the family.

BRIT MILAH[26]
for Dan Avi

As Dan is brought into the room, everyone says:

בָּרוּךְ הַבָּא בְּשֵׁם יְיָ.

Blessed are you who bear the divine presence.

Dan is handed from his great-grandmother, to his grandparents, to his eldest aunt and to his mother, who says:

My son, my child, you have been as dear to me as my own breath. May I hold you gently now with the love to keep you close and with the strength to let you grow.

She gives him to his father, who says:

My son, my child, a piece of my life is you. You have grown to life apart from me, but now I hold you close to my heart and cradle you in my arms with my love.

Parents:

We have been blessed with the gift of new life. We have shared love and pain and joy in bringing our son into life.

By the way we live, we aspire to teach our son to become a caring and loving person. We hope that in seeking to fulfill himself, he will accept his responsibilities to others and to his heritage. We rededicate ourselves to the creation of a Jewish home and to a life of compassion for others, hoping he will learn from our example.

God of our grandfathers, God of our grandmothers, we pray for covenant love, for life, for good. Keep us strong together.

בָּרוּךְ אַתָּה יְיָ, מְקוֹר הַחַיִּים מְשַׂמֵּחַ הַהוֹרִים עִם יַלְדֵיהֶם.

Blessed is the holy source of life, who causes parents to rejoice with their children.

Rabbi:

In Jewish folklore, Elijah is regarded as the one who announces the advent of the Messiah, the forerunner of messianic days. As we recall Elijah now, we rekindle our faith that every human life may yet bring about *y'mot hamoshiah,* the era of harmony and peace for all people.

Guests sing *Eliyahu Hanavi.* The *mohel* recites the blessing before performing the circumcision:

בָּרוּךְ אַתָּה יְיָ, אֱלֹהֵינוּ מֶלֶךְ הָעוֹלָם אֲשֶׁר קִדְּשָׁנוּ בְּמִצְוֹתָיו, וְצִוָּנוּ עַל הַמִּילָה.

Blessed by the Presence Whose sanctity fills our lives, we fulfill the mitzvah of circumcision.

Parents:

בָּרוּךְ אַתָּה יְיָ, אֱלֹהֵינוּ מֶלֶךְ הָעוֹלָם אֲשֶׁר קִדְּשָׁנוּ בְּמִצְוֹתָיו, וְצִוָּנוּ לְהַכְנִיסוֹ בִּבְרִיתוֹ שֶׁל אַבְרָהָם אָבִינוּ.

Blessed by the Presence Whose sanctity fills our lives, we bring our son into the covenant of Abraham our father.

All present say:

As he has been brought into the covenant of our people, so may he attain the blessings of Torah, *huppah* and a life of good deeds.

Raising the cup of wine, the rabbi says:

בָּרוּךְ אַתָּה יְיָ, אֱלֹהֵינוּ מֶלֶךְ הָעוֹלָם, בּוֹרֵא פְּרִי הַגָּפֶן.

בָּרוּךְ אַתָּה יְיָ, אֱלֹהֵינוּ מֶלֶךְ הָעוֹלָם אֲשֶׁר קִדֵּשׁ יְדִיד מִבֶּטֶן, וְחֹק בִּשְׁאֵרוֹ שָׂם, וְצֶאֱצָאָיו חָתַם בְּאוֹת בְּרִית קֹדֶשׁ. עַל כֵּן בִּשְׂכַר זֹאת, אֵל חַי, חֶלְקֵנוּ צוּרֵנוּ, צַוֵּה לְהַצִּיל יְדִידוּת שְׁאֵרֵנוּ מִשַּׁחַת. לְמַעַן בְּרִיתוֹ אֲשֶׁר שָׂם בִּבְשָׂרֵנוּ. בָּרוּךְ אַתָּה יְיָ, כּוֹרֵת הַבְּרִית.

אֱלֹהֵינוּ וֵאלֹהֵי אֲבוֹתֵינוּ, וְאִמּוֹתֵינוּ, קַיֵּם אֶת הַיֶּלֶד הַזֶּה לְאָבִיו וּלְאִמּוֹ, וְיִקָּרֵא שְׁמוֹ, בְּיִשְׂרָאֵל   בֶּן   . יִשְׂמַח הָאָב בְּיוֹצֵא חֲלָצָיו, וְתָגֵל אִמּוֹ בִּפְרִי בִטְנָהּ. כַּכָּתוּב: יִשְׂמַח אָבִיךָ וְאִמֶּךָ, וְתָגֵל יוֹלַדְתֶּךָ. וְנֶאֱמַר: וָאֶעֱבֹר עָלַיִךְ וָאֶרְאֵךְ מִתְבּוֹסֶסֶת בְּדָמָיִךְ, וָאֹמַר לָךְ בְּדָמַיִךְ חֲיִי, וָאֹמַר לָךְ בְּדָמַיִךְ חֲיִי. וְנֶאֱמַר: זָכַר לְעוֹלָם בְּרִיתוֹ, דָּבָר צִוָּה לְאֶלֶף דּוֹר. אֲשֶׁר כָּרַת אֶת אַבְרָהָם, וּשְׁבוּעָתוֹ לְיִצְחָק. וַיַּעֲמִידֶהָ לְיַעֲקֹב לְחֹק, לְיִשְׂרָאֵל בְּרִית עוֹלָם. וְנֶאֱמַר. וַיָּמָל אַבְרָהָם אֶת יִצְחָק בְּנוֹ, בֶּן שְׁמֹנַת יָמִים, כַּאֲשֶׁר צִוָּה אֹתוֹ אֱלֹהִים. הוֹדוּ לַייָ כִּי טוֹב, כִּי לְעוֹלָם חַסְדּוֹ. הוֹדוּ לַייָ כִּי טוֹב, כִּי לְעוֹלָם חַסְדּוֹ.   זֶה הַקָּטָן גָּדוֹל יִהְיֶה. כְּשֵׁם שֶׁנִּכְנַס לַבְּרִית, כֵּן יִכָּנֵס לְתוֹרָה, וּלְחֻפָּה, וּלְמַעֲשִׂים טוֹבִים.

Blessed is the Presence Whose sanctity fills our lives and ripens fruit on the vine.

You have sanctified your beloved from the womb, establishing your holy covenant throughout the generations. May devotion to the covenant continue to sustain us as a people. Blessed by the Presence Whose sanctity fills our lives, we give thanks for the covenant.

God of all life, sustain this child and let him be known in Israel as Dan Avi, son of Moshe and Avigail.

May the father rejoice in his offspring and the mother be glad with her children. May you teach him through word and deed the meaning of the covenant forever, the word commanded to a thousand generations, the covenant made with Abraham, Isaac, Jacob, Sarah, Rebecca, Rachel and Leah, and eternal covenant for Israel. As it is said, "And Abraham circumcised his son when he was eight days old, as God commanded." Give thanks to God for what is good, for covenant love that endures forever.

May this little child, Dan Avi ben Moshe v'Avigail, grow into manhood as a blessing to his family, the Jewish people and humanity. As he has entered the covenant of our people, so may he grow into a life of Torah, *huppah* and good deeds.

Parents drink from the wine which the baby has already tasted. They explain for whom Dan is named.

The rabbi recites the threefold priestly benediction. Then parents and all family members recite the *shehehiyanu*.

BRIT HABAT: WELCOMING OUR DAUGHTERS

"Go out and see what the Jews are doing."

The Babylonian Talmud[27]

Jews all over the world are busily inventing ceremonies to celebrate the birth of their daughters. There ceremonies go by many names: *simchat bat* (joy of the daughter), *brit hayyim* (covenant of life), *brit kedusha* (covenant of sanctification), *brit bat Zion* (covenant for the daughter of Zion), *brit b'not Yisrael* (covenant for the daughters of Israel), *brit e'dut* (covenant of witnessing), *brit ohel* (covenant of the tent), *brit hanerot* (covenant of candles), *brit Sarah* (covenant of Sarah), *brit rehitzah* (covenant of washing), *brit mikvah* (covenant of immersion), *brit milah* (covenant of the word*), and *brit habat.*

And this is only a partial list! Every ceremony that gets written down (many are not) is passed along to other parents, who almost always revise and reshape it for their own use.

This ferment of liturgical creativity has a number of modern sources. In the 1970s, as Jewish feminists became parents, they confronted the fact that compared to the celebration for the birth

* *A play on the two homonymic Hebrew words for circumcision and word.*

of a boy, the arrival of a baby girl was barely acknowledged.* The determination to correct the imbalance in liberal Jewish practice was fueled by a deeply felt wish to express the joy of delivering a daughter, and it was given shape by the hands-on, home-style, learn-as-you-do Judaism that was just coming into its own. The 1960s spiritual growth and back-to-your-roots movements coupled with the outpouring of Jewish awareness provoked by the 1967 war and the *The Jewish Catalogs* were born, offering a nonthreatening menu-approach to Judaism and Jewish practice.[28]

What began in the early 1970s as a tentative, even fringy practice, is already mainstream. Indeed, most rabbi's manuals now include a naming or welcoming ceremony for daughters. With every passing year, *brit habat* becomes less experimental and more established. Jewish rites of passage for baby daughters are no longer a novelty in modern Orthodox circles, where the absence of *halachah* on the subject frees people to experiment with home celebrations.

Some predict that decades or even centuries from now, there will be one normative liturgy for *brit habat,* as there is for *brit milah*. However, it is just as likely that our great-great-grandchildren will continue to have a wealth of choices when they welcome daughters into the covenant and community of Israel. Perhaps the most useful analogy will be the ritual for the Passover seder. Even as it retains the distinctive stories, symbols and songs of Pesach, the *haggadah* is given new interpretations annually.

But it is not always easy being a pioneer. Although many *brit habat* ceremonies exist, few people have access to them. And while some rabbis have file folders filled with examples, not all new parents are synagogue-affiliated. This leaves a lot of people starting from scratch, frantically searching for models and sources at a time when time and energy are at a premium.

This chapter is a remedy for that particular panic. Here you

* *This is far more true in Ashkenazic than in Sephardic practice, as you will see below. However, most American Jews trace their ancestry and practice to Eastern Europe.*

will find a menu of possibilities: blessings, prayers, ideas, and symbols culled from many *brit habat* ceremonies, as well as an outline and sample rituals that will help you go out and do as the Jews are doing.

HISTORY

As new and novel as *brit habat* may seem, it does have a history, albeit one we often have to read between the lines. From that perspective, *brit habat* may be seen as a revival of ancient custom. The Torah records that all new mothers owed the Temple thanksgiving offerings in the same amounts and of the same kinds, regardless of their baby's sex. The offering was due thirty-three days after birth for a boy, sixty-six days later for a girl, the difference representing the number of days of ritual "impurity" following the birth of a male or female child.[29]

What happened during those thirty-three or sixty-six days of separation from the community is the stuff of *midrash*—the storytelling that fills in the spaces between words of Torah.[30] There may well have been ceremonies for baby daughters during those days apart, rites not shared with the menfolk and therefore not recorded. Similarly, there may well have been folk customs for naming, welcoming and blessing daughters throughout the undocumented history of Jewish women's lives.

These are mostly lost to us. What remains from the Yiddish folkways of Ashkenazic Jews is a word, *brisitzeh* (a feminine Yiddish form of *bris*), probably some sort of covenant ceremony.[31] *Hollekreish,* another naming ceremony based on non-Jewish folk customs, may have had more significance for daughters than we now realize.

What remains in Ashkenazic tradition, and thus most American practice, is the public naming of daughters in the synagogue. The father is called to the Torah during the week after his daughter's birth, on Shabbat or on any day there is a Torah service.

There, he offers the *mi she'beirach* blessing, an all-purpose special-occasion blessing in which his daughter's name is announced for the first time.

The *mi she'beirach* blessing for naming a girl is:

> May the One who blessed our fathers Abraham, Isaac, and Jacob, Moses and Aaron, David and Solomon, may He bless the mother ______________ and her newborn daughter, whose name in Israel shall be ______________. May they raise her for the marriage canopy and for a life of good deeds.[32]

After the traditional service, it is customary to serve refreshments. Often, the mother and baby do not attend. If she is there, however, the mother may say the *birkat hagomel,* the prayer of thanksgiving for having survived a life-threatening ordeal. (See page 120.)

SEPHARDIC CUSTOMS

Sephardic Jews count a wealth of rituals and customs to celebrate a daughter's birth. The traditional Sephardic prayerbook even includes a ceremony called *Seder zeved habat,* celebration for the gift of a daughter described further later.

Syrian Jews name daughters in the synagogue, where the congregation sings special songs of *pizmonim,* that relate to the birth of a daughter. A *kiddush* and *s'eudat* in honor of the baby's birth follow the service.[33]

Moroccan Jews name daughters at home. The rabbi holds the child, quotes from the Bible, and pronounces a *mi she'beirach* that lists the names of the matriarchs. In addition to the special songs associated with the celebration, the women raise their voices in ululations during the naming as an expression of joy.

The Jews of Spain have a home ceremony held after the mother has recovered, called *las fadas,* a word probably based on *hadas,* which means fairies. This celebration may be an adaptation of a non-Jewish custom of having a child blessed by various good fairies.[34]

In some communities, the baby is brought into the celebration on a pillow, dressed in a miniature bridal gown. The baby is passed from guest to guest as each one adds a blessing. When she reaches the rabbi's lap, he recites a blessing for her health and happiness. Verses from Song of Songs and special *pizmonim* are sung and a lavish feast follows.

SEDER ZEVED HABAT[35]

יוֹנָתִי בְּחַגְוֵי הַסֶּלַע בְּסֵתֶר הַמַּדְרֵגָה. הַרְאִינִי אֶת מַרְאַיִךְ הַשְׁמִיעִנִי אֶת קוֹלֵךְ. כִּי קוֹלֵךְ עָרֵב וּמַרְאֵיךְ נָאוֶה

אַחַת הִיא יוֹנָתִי תַמָּתִי אַחַת הִיא לְאִמָּהּ. בָּרָה הִיא לְיוֹלַדְתָּהּ רָאוּהָ בָנוֹת וַיְאַשְּׁרוּהָ. מְלָכוֹת וּפִילַגְשִׁים וַיְהַלְלוּהָ.

מִי שֶׁבֵּרַךְ שָׂרָה וְרִבְקָה רָחֵל וְלֵאָה. וּמִרְיָם הַנְּבִיאָה וַאֲבִיגַיִל. וְאֶסְתֵּר הַמַּלְכָּה בַּת אֲבִיחַיִל. הוּא יְבָרֵךְ אֶת הַיַּלְדָּה הַנְּעִימָה (הַזֹּאת)* בְּמַזָּל טוֹב וּבְשָׁעָה בְּרָכָה. וִיגַדְּלָהּ בִּבְרִיאוּת שָׁלוֹם וּמְנוּחָה. וּתְזַכֶּה אֶת אָבִיהָ וְאֶת אִמָּהּ לִרְאוֹת בְּשִׂמְחָתָהּ וּבְחוּפָּתָהּ. בְּבָנִים וּבְבָנוֹת עֹשֶׁר וְכָבוֹד. דְּשֵׁנִים וְרַעֲנַנִּים יְנוּבוּן בְּשֵׂיבָה. וְכֵן יְהִי רָצוֹן וְנֹאמַר אָמֵן.

Oh my dove in the rocky clefts,
In the shelter of terrace high
Let me see your face
Let me hear your voice
For your voice is sweet
And your face is beautiful.

* *If the baby is present.*

If the baby is a first-born, add:

One alone is my dove, my perfect one,
The darling of her mother,

The delight of her who bore her.
Daughters saw her—they acclaimed her,
Queens and consorts—they sang her praises.

May the one who blessed our mothers, Sarah, Rebecca, Rachel and Leah, Miriam the prophetess, Abigail and Esther the queen, bless also this darling baby ______________. May the One bless her to grow up in comfort, health and happiness. May the One give to her parents the joy of seeing her happily married, a radiant mother of children, rich in honor and joy to a ripe old age. May this be the will of God, and let us say, Amen.

NEW TRADITIONS

Although there are precedents, there are no rules for *brit habat*. Your choices begin with the basics, starting with where and when.

Brit habat takes place at home or in the synagogue and there are pros and cons for both. You might choose a sanctuary or social hall for the space and because you want this to be a community celebration. Some people find it simpler to hire a caterer and keep the commotion out of the house.

But others feel that home is the only place for a family occasion like *brit habat*. It may be easier for you to care for the baby, reassure older siblings and host a celebration in the comfort of your own home.

Generally, parents schedule a *brit habat* on a day that is convenient for family and friends, and when the mother and baby can be present. Various intervals are used and justified on traditional grounds.

Eight days: Having the ceremony on the eighth day mirrors the ancient rite of *brit milah*. The same traditional explanations apply: the sanctity associated with the number eight, and the spiritual strength the baby derives from her first contact with Shabbat. Also, on the eighth day the miracle of birth is still very fresh in the parents' minds and the ceremony resounds with the primal emotions of labor and delivery. However, since mothers often don't feel ready for a party so soon after giving birth, the eighth day is a relatively infrequent choice for *brit habat.*

Fourteen days has been advanced as another interval with traditional roots. In the Torah, after the birth of a daughter a mother's ritual impurity ends after fourteen days. Two weeks allows for the mother's recovery and, according to some pediatricians, is a reasonable amount of time to keep a newborn away from crowds.

Thirty days is a popular choice since it allows the family enough time to recover, plan, and invite. It too has a basis in tradition, since the rabbis believed a child was only viable after thirty days. (See the section on *pidyon haben/habat.*)

Rosh hodesh: Some parents schedule the ceremony on the first day of the new moon. A day for new beginnings, *rosh hodesh* is traditionally associated with women, whose cycles reflect lunar cycles, and for whom it is a holiday.

Shabbat: Many families schedule *brit habat* on the Sabbath a few weeks or a month after the baby's birth. Since Shabbat itself is a covenant between God and Israel, it seems an appropriate time for a covenental ceremony. A *brit habat* on Shabbat can take place at different times in the day and in a number of contexts.

In many Reform congregations, the custom is to bring the baby to Friday night service where the rabbi adds a brief ceremony to the service, usually inviting the parents to bring the baby up to the *bimah.* Blessings are offered and the name is announced. In some synagogues it is the *minhag* (custom) to invite anyone present to add wishes and blessings for the baby. The Oneg Shabbat after services is commonly sponsored either by the new parents, or in the family's honor.

There are a number ways to incorporate *brit habat* into Shabbat morning services. The most obvious is by expanding the traditional *mi she'beirach* given above. In liberal congregations, both the father and mother go up to the *bimah* with the baby and other readings might follow the blessing. This kind of celebration has to be quite brief, however, so as not to disrupt the service.

Another option is to hold the ceremony immediately following the morning service, preceding *kiddush.* The *s'eudat mitzvah* can coincide with the Shabbat midday meal, either in the synagogue or at home.

Another popular setting for *brit habat* is the twilight peace of *havdalah,* the ceremony that separates Shabbat from the rest of the week, the mundane from the holy. *Havdalah brit habat* marks a separation in the baby's life too. Her recent transition from the womb into life is recalled and her entrance into the community of Israel is marked.

Once you've settled on where and when, there is the question of whom to invite and involve. As in all Jewish rites of passage, the preferred approach is to have as many people attend and participate as possible. While some parents mail invitations to their daughters' *brit habat* ceremonies, invitation is most commonly by word of mouth.

When *brit habat* takes place at home, the baby's parents usually lead the ceremony. When it is held in a synagogue, the rabbi officiates—although often with a great deal of parental participation. Many people have remarked that it seems appropriate for the *mesader,* the leader of the ceremony, to be a woman of learning and stature.

In general, it is a *mitzvah* to include as many people as possible in any ritual like this. Grandparents are usually given the most important *kibbudim* or honors, often with the honorary roles and titles from *brit milah—kvatterin, kvatter,* and *sandek.* The *sandek* (or *sandeket*) holds the baby during the naming.

Blessings, poems, readings or prayers—prepared by you or others—can be distributed to as many guests as you choose. Others can be honored with tasks like reciting the *motzi,* the blessing over bread (traditionally a braided challah) before the meal, or holding a prayer shawl over the *brit habat* (see *Hiddur Mitzvah:* Beautiful Touches).

Elijah's chair, which has been a well-established feature of *brit milah* since the Middle Ages, is now often included in *brit habat* as well. The *kisei shel Eliyahu* invokes the presence of the prophet, angel, protector of children, peripatetic guest and harbinger of *y'mot mashiach,* the days of the Messiah.

ELEMENTS OF THE CEREMONY

Of the hundreds of *brit habat* ceremonies in circulation, some are short and simple, others are long and elaborate. Although the ceremonies that appear at the end of this chapter give you an idea of their range, it is impossible to reproduce all the varieties and variations. However, a few elements seem nearly universal.

Brit habat tends to have a four part structure. The introductory section begins with the greeting *b'rucha haba'a,* and usually includes prayers or readings by the parents and/or rabbi. *Kiddush* is often recited here as well.

The second part is about covenant. Using blessings and/or symbolic actions, a baby daughter is entered into the covenanted people of Israel. Generally, this is followed by the threefold wish that she will also take on the *mitzvot* of Torah, *huppah,* and righteous actions.

The baby's name is announced and explained in the third section; her namesake(s) are recalled and sometimes an acrostic based on the letters of her name is recited. This is often followed by more blessings, prayers, readings, and wishes from the guests. The ceremony often ends with *shehehiyanu* and/or the priestly benediction.

The last part of *brit habat* is the celebratory meal and party, the *s'eudat mitzvah.**

** This outline is offered as a guide to help you organize your ceremony. Use it and change it as you like.*

The following "menu" explains some of the more common elements of *brit habat.** Be advised, however, that Jewish rituals are traditionally as powerful as they are brief. If you include every last item on this menu in your *brit habat,* your "meal" will be too rich—and the ceremony will go on too long.

INTRODUCTION *Brucha haba'a.* Blessed is she who enters. This greeting begins virtually all *brit habat* ceremonies. It recalls *brit milah,* where *baruch haba* (blessed is he who enters) begins the ritual, and it also acknowledges the divinity of the female.

Candle lighting can make a beautiful beginning. A tradition associated with *brit milah,* lighting candles has an added dimension at a *brit habat* because the *mitzvah* of lighting Shabbat candles is given to women.

There are many ways to incorporate candles into a *brit habat.* The mother can light a single braided *havdalah* candle or a pair of white Shabbat candles. Or the female members of the family or all the women guests may be invited to bring their Shabbat candlesticks and light them together (traditional white or a rainbow of colored candles, as you wish).

The baby's mother or her parents may light tapers in a pair of holders that are a gift to their daughter. If the baby is named for a female relative who has died, her candlesticks might be used. (See *Hiddur Mitzvah:* Beautiful Touches.)

This blessing is one of several used for candle lighting at *brit habat*:

בָּרוּךְ אַתָּה יְיָ, אֱלֹהֵינוּ מֶלֶךְ הָעוֹלָם אֲשֶׁר קִדְּשָׁנוּ בְּמִצְוֹתָיו, וְצִוָּנוּ עַל קִדּוּשׁ הַחַיִּים.

Baruch ata Adonai Elohenu melech ha'olam asher kidshanu b'mitzvotav vitsivanu al kiddush ha hayyim.

You are blessed, Adonai of all creation, by whose mitzvot we are hallowed, who commands us to sanctify life.

* *Remember that other chapters in this book contain examples and suggestions that apply to* brit habat.

Introductory Readings and Prayers: As the examples at the end of this chapter illustrate, the first readings and poems set the tone, and often explain the "theology" of the ceremony.

This story from the *Midrash* begins many *brit habat* ceremonies:

> When Israel stood to receive the Torah, the Holy One, Blessed be the One, said to them: I am giving you my Torah. Present to me good guarantors that you will guard it, and I shall give it to you.
>
> They said: Our ancestors are our guarantors.
>
> The Holy One, Blessed be the One, said, Your ancestors are not sufficient guarantors. Yet bring me good guarantors and I shall give you the Torah.
>
> They said, Master of the Universe, our prophets are our guarantors.
>
> The One said to them, The prophets are not sufficient guarantors. Yet bring me good guarantors and I shall give you the Torah.
>
> They said, Our children are our guarantors.
>
> And the Holy One, Blessed be the One, said, They certainly are good guarantors. For their sake, I give the Torah to you.[36]

Kiddush: The blessing and drinking of wine is a part of virtually every Jewish celebration. After the blessing, the baby is given a drop to drink. The cup can then be passed to the parents, grandparents, and other guests. The *kiddush* cup can be given special attention and mention, especially if it is the cup the parents used at their wedding, or if it is a special gift to the baby.

בָּרוּךְ אַתָּה יְיָ, אֱלֹהֵינוּ מֶלֶךְ הָעוֹלָם, בּוֹרֵא פְּרִי הַגָּפֶן.

> *Baruch ata Adonai Eloheynu Melech Ha-olam borey p'ri hagafen.*
>
> Holy One of Blessing, Your Presence fills creation, forming the fruit of the vine.

COVENANT Daughters are most commonly entered into the covenant with a *b'racha,* a blessing, such as this one:

בָּרוּךְ אַתָּה יְיָ, אֱלֹהֵינוּ מֶלֶךְ הָעוֹלָם אֲשֶׁר קִדֵּשׁ יְדִיד הַבֶּטֶן. אֵל חַי חֶלְקֵנוּ צוּרֵנוּ, צַוֵּה לְהַצִּיל יְדִידוּת שְׁאֵרֵנוּ מִשַּׁחַת, לְמַעַן בְּרִיתוֹ. בָּרוּךְ אַתָּה יְיָ כּוֹרֵת הַבְּרִית.
אֱלוֹהַ כָּל הַבְּרִיאוֹת קַיֵּם אֶת הַיַּלְדָּה הַזֹּאת לְאָבִיהָ וּלְאִמָּהּ.

You have sanctified your beloved from the womb establishing Your holy convenant throughout the generations. May devotion to the covenant continue to sustain us as a people. Praised are You, Eternal God, who has established the covenant. Blessed by the Presence whose sanctity fills our lives, we give thanks for the covenant.[37]

Many parents feel that *brit habat* requires symbolic action as well as words. Proposals for a ritual drawing of blood to parallel *brit milah* never met with success.[38] Instead, water has become the most popular covenental symbol for *brit habat*. Washing the baby, most commonly just her feet or hands, is an earthy yet gentle physical act that seems to have struck a responsive chord among liberal American Jews, who have incorporated it into a range of *brit habat* ceremonies. Since its publication in 1983, *brit rehitzah,* the covenant of washing, has become a primary source and a touchstone for countless other ceremonies.[39]

Although some people are disconcerted by the similarity between washing and Christian baptism, water rituals are very much a part of Jewish practice. Indeed, observant Jews wash their hands and say a blessing before meals, and *mikvah* marks the cycles of women's lives. The Talmud even suggests that as Abram became Abraham through the covenant or circumcision, Sarai became Sarah through *mikvah.*

The Torah is rich with water imagery, much of it associated with women. Sarah and Abraham welcomed the three guests who brought them news of their son, by bringing them water for washing. Rebecca makes her biblical appearance at a well—as does Rachel. Miriam the prophetess, sister of Moses and Aaron, is associated with a well of living water that sustained the Hebrews in the wilderness.[40]

The covenental ritual act of *brit rehitzah* is the parents' washing their daughter's feet. As in *brit milah* there is a blessing before the act of covenant, and another afterward: *

Before the washing, the rabbi or *mesader habrit* says:

בָּרוּךְ אַתָּה יְיָ, אֱלֹהֵינוּ מֶלֶךְ הָעוֹלָם זוֹכֵר הַבְּרִית.

Baruch ata Adonai Eloheynu Melech Ha-olam zocher habrit.

Blessed are You, Adonai our God, Ruler of the Universe, Who is mindful of the covenant.

After the washing the parents say:

בָּרוּךְ אַתָּה יְיָ, אֱלֹהֵינוּ מֶלֶךְ הָעוֹלָם זוֹכֵר הַבְּרִית בִּרְחִיצַת רַגְלַיִם.

Baruch ata Adonai Eloheynu Melech Ha-olam zocher habrit b'rechitzat raglayim.

Blessed are You, Adonai our God, Ruler of the Universe, Who is mindful of the covenant through the washing of the feet.

The threefold wish, traditional to *brit milah,* usually follows the convenantal prayer or ritual. It expresses the communal wish that this daughter will fulfill the three requirements of all Jews, now that she has become a member of the people of Israel.

כְּשֵׁם שֶׁנִּכְנַס לַבְּרִית, כֵּן יִכָּנֵס לְתוֹרָה וּלְחֻפָּה וּלְמַעֲשִׂים טוֹבִים.

K'shem she-nich-n'sah la-brit.
Ken ti-kanes l'torah ul'chupah ul'ma-asim tovim.

* *The song "Mayyim" is a wonderful accompaniment to any ceremony that involves water; you might want to have your guests hum the melody during the washing.*

As she has entered the covenant, so may she enter a life devoted to Torah, *huppah* and the accomplishment of good deeds.

A commentary on these wishes appears in countless *brit habat* ceremonies:

We dedicate our child to Torah—to a never-ending fascination with study and learning. With a book she will never be alone.

We dedicate our child to *huppah*—to never-ending growth as a human being, capable of giving and receiving love. With loving family and friends she will never be alone.

We dedicate our child to *ma-asim tovim*—to a never-ending concern for family and community, justice and charity. While she cares for others, she will never be alone.[41]

THE NAME, READINGS, AND CONCLUSION Traditionally, the naming of a daughter occurs in the context of the *mi she'beirach* (see above). While this formula is not used in all *brit habat* ceremonies, nearly all pay a great deal of attention to the baby's name.

Anything you say about how you chose your daughter's name will be meaningful. Since most American Jews name children to honor the memory of a family member who has died, the loved one is often described and remembered. The Hebrew and/or biblical meaning of many names suggest wonderful commentaries as well.

There is an old custom of making an acrostic poem using the first letters of the baby's name in Hebrew. Each letter is matched with a phrase or line from the Bible that also begins with that letter. The most common source for this is Psalm 119, but you can also try Song of Songs, Proverbs, other Psalms, and the weekly Torah portion closest to your baby's birth. Sometimes, acrostics are made into beautiful wall-hangings using calligraphy.

One acrostic for a baby named Rachel is:

רַבּוֹת בָּנוֹת עָשׂוּ חָיִל, וְאַתְּ עָלִית עַל כֻּלָּנָה

Many daughters have done virtuously, but you have outdone them all. (Proverbs 31:29)

חֶסֶד וֶאֱמֶת אַל יַעַזְבֻךָ קָשְׁרֵם עַל גַּרְגְּרוֹתֶיךָ כָּתְבֵם עַל לוּחַ לִבֶּךָ

Let not loyal love and truth forsake you; bind them around your neck; inscribe them on the tablet of your heart. (Proverbs 3:3)

לְכוּ נְרַנְּנָה לַה׳ נָרִיעָה לְצוּר יִשְׁעֵנוּ.

Let us go to sing to God; let us shout joyfully to the rock of our salvation. (Psalm 95:1)

Blessings, prayers, poems, wishes and readings are often included here. Obviously, original writings and songs of all kinds make a powerful addition. Among the traditional blessings that are used are: *birkat hagomel,* the blessing said after recovery from an illness (see page 120); and *ha-tov ve-hamativ,* another traditional prayer recited on the occasion of a great blessing (page 35).

The biblical poem *Shir haShirim,* Song of Songs, is often quoted at *brit habat* ceremonies, as it is at weddings.[42] And some couples use the theme of the seven wedding blessings, the *sheva brachot,* choosing *brachot* from the wedding liturgy and other sources. (An example appears below). In the same vein, some parents include a song or reading from their wedding.

Siblings old enough to participate might say a few words of their own choosing. And these lines are especially powerful when spoken by grandparents:

The crown of the aged are children's children
And the glory of children are their parents. (Proverbs 17:6)

In the Talmud there is the story of an old man who was seen planting a carob tree as the king rode by. "Old man," the king called, "how many years will it be before that tree bears fruit?" The old man replied, "Perhaps seventy years." The king asked, "Do you really expect to be alive to eat the fruit of that tree?"

"No," answered the old man. "But just as I found the world fruitful when I was born, so I plant trees that later generations may eat thereof." (Ta'anit 23a)

Whoever teaches his child does not teach his child alone, but also his descendants and so on to the end of all generations. (Kiddushin 30a)

To involve more of your guests in the ceremony, invite the company to offer their prayers and wishes for your new baby: May she live to be 120; May her life be filled with laughter and people who love her; May she sleep through the night soon.

If the group is small enough, and the baby placid, you could even pass her from person to person as they speak. (And make sure the tape recorder is on!)

The end of the ceremony is signaled by the following three prayers (in any combination):

Shehehiyanu: This prayer of thanksgiving may be the most common element of all *brit habat* ceremonies. Its familiar melody and associations with happy occasions always evoke an enthusiastic response:

בָּרוּךְ אַתָּה יְיָ, אֱלֹהֵינוּ מֶלֶךְ הָעוֹלָם שֶׁהֶחֱיָנוּ וְקִיְּמָנוּ וְהִגִּיעָנוּ לַזְּמַן הַזֶּה:

Baruch ata Adonai, Elohenu Melech Ha-olam
shehehiyanu vikiamanu vihigianu lazman hazeh.

Holy One of Blessing, Your Presence fills creation,
You have kept us alive
You have sustained us
You have brought us to this moment.

Traditional blessing for a daughter: On Friday night, after the Shabbat blessings are made, families add a blessing for their children. Reciting these words for the first time at *brit habat* can be a wonderful experience:

יְשִׂמֵךְ אֱלֹהִים כְּשָׂרָה רִבְקָה רָחֵל וְלֵאָה:

Yaseemech Eloheem k'Sara, Rivka, Rachel v'Leah.

May God make you as Sarah, Rebecca, Rachel and Leah.

Some families add the names of grandmothers and great-grandmothers to the list of matriarchs.

The *priestly benediction* concludes all sorts of Jewish rituals and services, and some parents include it in the Shabbat blessing of their children. If a rabbi is officiating, he or she most often recites this. If not, the parents or the entire company can repeat these words for the baby:

יְבָרֶכְךָ יְיָ וְיִשְׁמְרֶךָ,
יָאֵר יְיָ פָּנָיו אֵלֶיךָ וִיחֻנֶּךָּ,
יִשָּׂא יְיָ פָּנָיו אֵלֶיךָ וְיָשֵׂם לְךָ שָׁלוֹם.

May God bless you and protect you
May God's presence shine for you and be favorable to you
May God's face turn to you and give you peace.

A rousing chorus of *Siman Tov Umazel Tov* ends the ceremony and signals the beginning of the *simcha*—the party.

S'EUDAT MITZVAH According to Jewish law, major life-cycle events are celebrated with a *s'eudat mitzvah.* These meals begin with the traditional blessing over challah and end with the *birkat hamazon,* the prayers sung upon completion of a meal. Because *brit habat* ceremonies are still relatively new, and because many of the guests at such celebrations (Jews and non-Jews alike) may not be familiar with the prayers and symbols you select, many parents prepare a printed "guide" to the proceedings. (For more about planning a *s'eudat mitzvah* and booklets, see "Simcha Means Party.")

Naming Ceremony for Shira Elizabeth[43]

Song: *Hava Nashira*

Barucha haba'a b'sheym Adonai.

May she who enters be blessed in the name of the Lord.

Through this covenant we affirm our daughter's part in the covenant, the *brit,* made between God and Israel at Mount Sinai. Our sources emphasize that the entire Jewish people, women and men, children and infants, born and unborn, were included in the revelation of the Law and in its affirmation. To understand this covenant and to live meaningfully by it has always been the central endeavor of each Jew in every generation. We give thanks for the opportunity to bring our daughter into the covenant and we say:

בָּרוּךְ אַתָּה יְיָ, אֱלֹהֵינוּ מֶלֶךְ הָעוֹלָם אֲשֶׁר קִדְּשָׁנוּ בְּמִצְוֹתָיו וְצִוָּנוּ לְהַכְנִיסָהּ בִּבְרִיתוֹ שֶׁל עַם יִשְׂרָאֵל. כְּשֵׁם שֶׁנִּכְנֶסֶת לִבְרִית כֵּן תִּכָּנְסִי לְתוֹרָה וּלְחוּפָּה וּלְמַעֲשִׂים טוֹבִים.

Blessed are you, Lord our God, Ruler of the universe who has made us holy through Your commandments and commanded us to bring our daughter into the covenant of Israel. As our daughter enters the covenant, so may she attain love of learning through the study of Torah, happiness in partnership with another human being, and the capacity to act toward others in honest, respectful and ethical ways.

At our marriage twelve years ago, seven blessings were recited. Today in celebration of our joy at the birth of our daughter, we ask loved ones to recite seven blessings over this *kiddush* cup filled with wine, the symbol of joy.

בָּרוּךְ אַתָּה יְיָ, אֱלֹהֵינוּ מֶלֶךְ הָעוֹלָם, בּוֹרֵא פְּרִי הַגָּפֶן.

Praised are You, Lord our God, Source of the universe, Creator of the fruit of the vine.

בָּרוּךְ אַתָּה יְיָ אֱלֹהֵינוּ מֶלֶךְ הָעוֹלָם יוֹצֵר הָאָדָם.

Praised are You, Lord our God, Source of the Universe, Creator of humanity.

בָּרוּךְ אַתָּה יְיָ אֱלֹהֵינוּ מֶלֶךְ הָעוֹלָם אֲשֶׁר יָצַר אֶת הָאָדָם בְּצַלְמוֹ, בְּצֶלֶם דְּמוּת תַּבְנִיתוֹ, וְהִתְקִין לוֹ מִמֶּנּוּ בִּנְיַן עֲדֵי עַד. בָּרוּךְ אַתָּה יְיָ, יוֹצֵר הָאָדָם.

Praised are You, Lord our God, Source of the universe, Who created human beings in Your image and Your likeness. And out of their very selves You prepared for them a perpetual spiritual being. Praised are You, our Lord, Creator of humanity.

בָּרוּךְ אַתָּה יְיָ אֱלֹהֵינוּ מֶלֶךְ הָעוֹלָם אֲשֶׁר קִדְּשָׁנוּ בְּמִצְוֹתָיו וְצִוָּנוּ עַל קִדּוּשׁ הַחַיִּים.

Praised are You, Lord our God, Source of the universe, Who commands us to sanctify Life.

בָּרוּךְ אַתָּה יְיָ אֱלֹהֵינוּ מֶלֶךְ הָעוֹלָם זוֹכֵר הַבְּרִית וְנֶאֱמָן בִּבְרִיתוֹ וְקַיָּם בְּמַאֲמָרוֹ.

Praised are You, Lord our God, Source of the universe, Who remembers the covenant and Who is steadfastly faithful in Your covenant, keeping Your promise.

בָּרוּךְ אַתָּה יְיָ מְשַׂמֵּחַ הוֹרִים עִם יַלְדֵיהֶם.

Praised are You, Lord our God, Source of the universe, Who causes parents to rejoice with their children.

בָּרוּךְ אַתָּה יְיָ אֱלֹהֵינוּ מֶלֶךְ הָעוֹלָם שֶׁהֶחֱיָנוּ וְקִיְּמָנוּ וְהִגִּיעָנוּ לַזְּמַן הַזֶּה

Praised are You, Lord our God, Source of the universe, for giving us life, for sustaining us, for enabling us to reach this day.

Mother:

This baby, Shira Elizabeth, is named in loving remembrance of my mother Shirley, and my grandmother Lillian. Both live in her. Let her life make her grandmother and her great-grandmother, unknown to her, known to all who see her.

May the One who blessed our Mothers, Sarah, Rebecca, Leah and Rachel, and our Fathers, Abraham, Isaac and Jacob, bless these parents and their newborn daughter. Her name shall be Shira Elizabeth. May her parents rear their daughter with love of Torah, and the performance of good deeds, and may they be privileged to bring her to the marriage canopy.
Let us say, Amen.

Priestly blessing:

Bread is the symbol of sustenance and honey the sign of sweetness. We dip the bread in honey in hope that our daily strivings will be sweetened by our love for each other.

בָּרוּךְ אַתָּה יְיָ, אֱלֹהֵינוּ מֶלֶךְ הָעוֹלָם הַמּוֹצִיא לֶחֶם מִן הָאָרֶץ:

Praised are You, Lord our God, Source of the universe, Who provides us with the staff of life.

BRIT SHOMREI HAMACHZORIM
Covenant of the Guardians of the Sacred Cycles[44]
for Adina Sara

In Jewish tradition, Elijah the Prophet represents the coming of the Messianic time. Elijah is present at the covenant whose sign is circumcision, at the Pesach seder, at the weekly *havdalah* ceremony; and he is known as the guardian of young children. The presence of Elijah at this covenant ceremony bids us look through the life of one child to the fulfillment of all life . . .

Adina Sara is brought to the chair of Elijah.

"When the men saw that Moses was so long in coming down from the mountain, they went to Aaron and asked him to make them a god. He said to them, 'Take off the gold rings that are on the ears of your wives, your sons, and your daughters, and bring them to me.'

"And the men took off the gold rings that were in their ears[45] too impatient to notice that the women refused their gold."

And so, the Holy Ancient One made the special relationship of women to *rosh hodesh*. Celebrating the new moon, women became guardians of the cycles of sacred time. They watched the light grow bright and diminish, and with the light, welcomed holy days and Shabbat days in their order. And the ebb and flow of the cycles within their bodies made them watchful, mindful of the gifts of heaven and earth.

Today, we publicly announce the birth of our new daughter and sister, welcoming her into this covenant our mothers have guarded in secret for so long. . . .

Ever since Avraham and Sarah began helping people to discover God, this has been our vision; a world of men and women acting together, sharing the tasks needed to nurture and to teach, to sustain and develop, that we reach the sacred time for which we wait.

בָּרוּךְ אַתָּה יְיָ, אֱלֹהֵינוּ מֶלֶךְ הָעוֹלָם שֶׁהֶחֱיָנוּ וְקִיְּמָנוּ וְהִגִּיעָנוּ לַזְּמַן הַזֶּה:

Let us bless the source of All who has breathed life into us, sustained us and brought us to this precious moment.

AWAKENING OF THE FIVE SENSES

Sight

The mother lights two Shabbat candles and says:[46]

Jewish women have been guardians of the light, kindling the spiritual flame for home and community since ancient times. With every Shabbat and holy day we remember the spark of spirit within, and manifest its beauty and wonder through lighting the fire of enlightenment, love and peace.

בָּרוּךְ אַתָּה יְיָ, אֱלֹהֵינוּ מֶלֶךְ הָעוֹלָם בּוֹרֵא מְאוֹרֵי הָאֵשׁ

Let us bless the source of All, who creates the illuminations of the flame.

Taste

Adina Sara is given a taste of wine as her father says:

Why do we make a blessing over wine rather than water? Water, after all, symbolizes purity and was created directly by God. Wine involves a partnership between people and God. God provides the fruit that we transform into wine, which in turn alters our awareness and lifts our spirit.[47]

May Adina Sara take what God provides and make it holy.

בָּרוּךְ אַתָּה יְיָ, אֱלֹהֵינוּ מֶלֶךְ הָעוֹלָם בּוֹרֵא פְּרִי הַגָּפֶן.

Let us bless the source of All, who creates the fruit of the vine, symbol of our rejoicing.

Sound

Adina Sara's mother introduces and then sings the Sarah *niggun,* a wordless melody, after which the guests all join in. She says:

May the sound of blessing caress her ears and fill her heart.

בָּרוּךְ אַתָּה יְיָ, אֱלֹהֵינוּ מֶלֶךְ הָעוֹלָם שׁוֹמֵעַ תְּפִלָּה.

Let us bless the source of All, who listens to prayer from the heart.

Smell

As Adina Sara is given flowers to smell:

The sense of smell unites us with our breath and reminds us of the soul. May the fragrance of beauty and peace surround Adina Sara as she remembers the wisdom of her soul.

בָּרוּךְ אַתָּה יְיָ, אֱלֹהֵינוּ מֶלֶךְ הָעוֹלָם בּוֹרֵא עִשְׂבֵי בְשָׂמִים.

Let us bless the source of All, who creates the sweet-smelling grasses.

Touch

As Adina Sara's hands are washed with water that was collected from rain, lake, river or sea water:

Brit is the covenant of our separate male and female realities, united and transformed by an awareness of Spirit.

With the purifying water from the Garden of Eden do we wash, wake and welcome you into the covenant of women, guarding the sacred cycles of time. From the Source of Oneness are we all born. Remember and return often to the pure spring of life. Immerse yourself in truth, joy and hope.

בָּרוּךְ אַתָּה יְיָ, אֱלֹהֵינוּ מֶלֶךְ הָעוֹלָם אֲשֶׁר קִדְּשָׁנוּ בְּמִצְוֹתָיו, וְצִוָּנוּ עַל נְטִילַת יָדָיִם.

Let us bless the source of All, who guides us on the path of holiness and directs us to lift up our hands through washing with water.

מִי שֶׁבֵּרַךְ אִמּוֹתֵינוּ שָׂרָה, רִבְקָה, רָחֵל וְלֵאָה
וּמִרְיָם הַנְּבִיאָה וַאֲבִיגַיִל, וְאֶסְתֵּר הַמַּלְכָּה בַּת אֲבִיחַיִל
הוּא יְבָרֵךְ אֶת הַנַּעֲרָה הַנְּעִימָה הַזֹּאת
וְיִקָּרֵא שְׁמָהּ בְּיִשְׂרָאֵל
בְּמַזַּל טוֹב וּבְשָׁעַת בְּרָכָה
וִיגַדְּלָהּ בִּבְרִיאוּת שָׁלוֹם וּמְנוּחָה
לְתוֹרָה וּלְחוּפָּה וּלְמַעֲשִׂים טוֹבִים
וְיִזְכּוּ אֶת אָבִיהָ וְאֶת אִמָּהּ לִרְאוֹת בְּשִׂמְחָתָהּ
בְּבָנִים וּבָנוֹת עוֹשֶׁר וְכָבוֹד
דְּשֵׁנִים וְרַעֲנַנִּים יְנוּבוּן בְּשֵׂיבָה
וְכֵן יְהִי רָצוֹן וְנֹאמַר אָמֵן.

May God who blessed our mothers
Sarah, Rebekah, Rachel, and Leah
Miriam the prophet and Avigayil
and Esther the Queen, daughter of Avihayil
bless this beautiful little girl
and let her name be called in Israel
______________ daughter of ______________
at this favorable moment of blessing.

May she be raised in health, peace, and tranquillity
To study Torah
To stand under the *huppah* (if that is her choice)
To do good deeds.
May her parents merit to see her happy
blessed with children, wealth, and honor
peaceful and content in their old age
May this be God's will
Amen.[48]

Parents explain the meaning of Adina Sara's name.

Let us bless the Source of all, who has brought us to a life of service, and given us the opportunity to introduce our daughter to the covenant of the sacred cycles.

Everyone sings: *Siman Tov Umazel Tov.*

BRIT OHEL SHEL SARAH IMEINU[49]
Covenant of the Tent of Sarah our Mother
for Rivka Yael

Song: *Ma to-vu*

How wonderful are your tents, Jacob
Your dwelling places Israel!

The baby is brought in and everyone says:

Brucha haba'a.

We welcome you into our midst
We greet you as you enter into the covenant of Israel.

As Abraham was father to the Jewish people, so Sarah was its mother. Our sages say, Abraham dealt with the men and Sarah dealt with the women.

Abraham would bring men into relationship with God and his people through *milah* and the covenant of religious circumcision. Sarah would bring the women into relationship with God and her people through their coming into her tent and taking formal residence there.

In Sarah's name, we now perform this ceremony of *brit ohel,* and bring this daughter of the Jewish people into her tent and into the covenant of Sarah our mother.

We thank you Adonai, our God and universal Sovereign, Who has made us holy by means of the *mitzvot,* commanding us regarding the covenant of the tent.

The *sandeket,* the baby's maternal grandmother, is seated in the center of the room. Four friends raise a large, colorful silk scarf over her head. The parents hand the baby to the *sandeket* and say:

בָּרוּךְ אַתָּה יְיָ אֱלֹהֵינוּ מֶלֶךְ הָעוֹלָם, אֲשֶׁר קִדְּשָׁנוּ בְּמִצְוֹתָיו וְצִוָּנוּ לְהַכְנִיסָהּ לִבְרִיתָהּ שֶׁל שָׂרָה אִמֵּנוּ.

We are grateful to You, Adonai, for You are our God and Ruler of the Universe. You have made us holy by means of the *mitzvot,* commanding us to bring our daughter into the covenant of Sarah our mother.

Everyone together:

כְּשֵׁם שֶׁנִּכְנְסָה לַבְּרִית. כֵּן תִּכָּנֵס לְתוֹרָה וּלְחוּפָּה וּלְמַעֲשִׂים טוֹבִים.

As she has entered into the covenant, so may she enter into Torah, *huppah* and a life of good deeds.

The *sandeket* is given the scarf; she wraps it around the baby and hands her back to her mother:

בָּרוּךְ אַתָּה יְיָ, אֱלֹהֵינוּ מֶלֶךְ הָעוֹלָם, בּוֹרֵא פְּרִי הַגָּפֶן.

We praise you, Adonai, our God and universal Ruler, who creates the fruit of the vine.

בָּרוּךְ אַתָּה יְיָ אֱלֹהֵינוּ מֶלֶךְ הָעוֹלָם, אֲשֶׁר קִדֵּשׁ אֶת הָאוֹהֶל וְכָל הַנִּכְנָסִים בּוֹ תַּפְרִיחַ אוֹהֶל צַדִּיקִים שֶׁנֵּדַע כִּי שָׁלוֹם הוּא. בָּרוּךְ אַתָּה יְיָ מוֹשִׁיבֵנוּ בְּאוֹהָלִים.

We praise you Adonai, our God and Ruler, who has sanctified the tent and all who enter it. Cause the tent of the righteous to flourish, that we may know that it is all peace. We are grateful to you Adonai, for making us dwell in tents.

Eloheynu, our God and our ancestor's God, sustain this child who is to be known in Israel as Rivka Yael and referred to in the world as Ruth Joyce.

Parents:

Help us to nurture her and encourage her to fulfill the blessing in her name.

Company:

May her mother and father rejoice and find delight in their daughter,
Let her coming into the covenant of the tent be at a favorable time for God and for Israel.

Parents:

May we, her parents, find joy in this moment and pleasure in all that she becomes.
May our tiny daughter grow to be great.

The priestly benediction, concluding:

May Adonai turn to each of you
and to all of us
and make for us a life
of wholeness and hopefulness and peace.
Amen.

Song: *Siman Tov Umazel Tov*

BRIT E'DUT
The Covenant of Witnessing[50]
for Sarah Beth

We have come together today to welcome our new daughter into our family and into the covenant of the Jewish people. Over 3000 years ago, our ancestors stood at Mount Sinai and entered into a covenant with God. Men, women, children, officers, elders, hewers of wood and drawers of water all stood before the Lord and proclaimed:

כָּל־הַדְּבָרִים אֲשֶׁר־דִּבֶּר יְהוָה נַעֲשֶׂה׃

All the words the Lord has spoken we will do.

The covenant which was established at Sinai was made not only with our ancestors but with those who would follow. This covenant has been reaffirmed throughout the millennia.

Today we too are gathered; men, women and children, our heads and our elders and a drawer of water; for Sarah, as she came into the world, drew out of her mother the waters that had sustained her before her birth.

We too, through our words today, with this drawer of water in our midst, reaffirm the pledge of our ancestors:

כֹּל אֲשֶׁר־דִּבֶּר יְהוָה נַעֲשֶׂה וְנִשְׁמָע׃

All that the Lord has spoken we will do and obey.

Everyone says:

Brucha haba'a.

May she who comes before us today be blessed.

When Abraham and Sarah dwelt at Mamre, three men appeared at the door of their tent. As a sign of hospitality, they offered these travelers water to drink and to wash their feet. In the same way that Abraham and Sarah welcomed the travelers, so do we welcome Sarah into this world, with food and drink and the washing of her feet.

Everyone sings *shehehiyanu.*

Father:

Sarah, as you begin your journey through life, we pray that you will find sustenance in *mayim hayyim,* the living waters which Judaism offers to all who draw from the well of our tradition.

Sarah's feet are washed.

Mother:

As your father and I stood under the shelter of this *tallis* to be joined together as husband and wife, so now do we encircle you within it as you enter the circle of our family. As we wrap you in this *tallis,* so may your life be wrapped in justice and righteousness. As we embrace you today, so may you embrace your tradition and your people.

As your eyes are filled with wonder when you gaze at the world, so too may you be filled with wonder at the everyday miracles of life.

As you startle to the world around you, so may you remain ever open both to the happiness and to the pain of those you encounter in the world.

As you cry for food and comfort now, so may you one day cry out to correct the injustices of the world, to help clothe the naked and feed the hungry.

As your hand tightly grasps your mother's finger, so may you grasp hold of learning and grow in knowledge and in wisdom.

"Every person born into this world, represents something new, something that never existed before, something original and unique. It is the duty of every person in Israel to know and consider that she is unique in the world, in her particular character, and that there has never been anyone like her in the world."[51]

אֱלֹהֵינוּ וֵאלֹהֵי אִמּוֹתֵינוּ, קַיֵּם אֶת הַיַּלְדָּה הַזֹּאת לְאָבִיהָ וּלְאִמָּהּ, וְיִקָּרֵא שְׁמוֹ, בְּיִשְׂרָאֵל . . . יִשְׂמַח הָאָב בְּיוֹצֵאת חֲלָצָיו, וְתָגֵל אִמּוֹ בִּפְרִי בִטְנָהּ. זֹאת הַקְּטַנָּה גְּדוֹלָה תִּהְיֶה. כְּשֵׁם שֶׁנִּכְנְסָה לַבְּרִית, כֵּן תִּכָּנֵס לְתוֹרָה, וּלְחֻפָּה, וּלְמַעֲשִׂים טוֹבִים.

Oh God, God of all generations, sustain this child and let her be known in the house of Israel as Sarah Batya bat Yakov v'Devorah. May our daughter bring us joy and happiness in the months and years to come. As we have brought her into the covenant of Torah today, so may she enter into the study of

Torah, the blessings of marriage and the performance of good deeds.

Sarah's namesakes are remembered.

Grandparents:

Our God and God of all generations, we are grateful for new beginnings, for the bond of new life that links one generation to another. Thankful for the blessings of family, for the love and care that bring meaning and happiness to our lives, we rejoice with our children at the birth of their child, our grandchild.

May they grow together as a family in health and in strength, in harmony, wisdom and love, their home filled with words of Torah and acts of kindness.

May we be enabled to share in the joy of seeing this child grow into adulthood, a blessing to her family, her people and all humanity.

All recite the priestly benediction and *kiddush*.

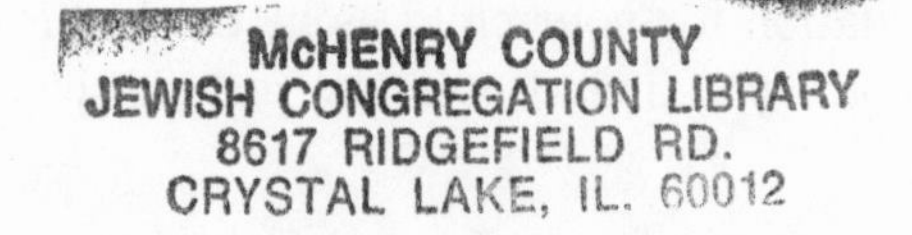

HIDDUR MITZVAH: BEAUTIFUL TOUCHES

According to the rabbinic principle of *hiddur mitzvah,* when a physical object is needed to fulfill a commandment, the object should be made as beautiful as possible. In the past, even the clamps and knives used for *brit milah* were richly decorated.

Beautifying the ceremonies of birth seems a natural expression of the joy surrounding a new baby. Since there are fewer communal traditions and objects for enhancing personal celebrations these days, some families have retrieved customs from the past to fulfill the commandment and also the human urge for *hiddur mitzvah.*

Whatever objects you use and save will become family heirlooms that will recall powerful memories for you and hold a special fascination for your child as he or she grows. Whatever songs and words you include will always be magic.

OBJECTS

CANDLES Although the presence of candles at a *brit milah* is common in Jewish communities around the world, it is unfamiliar to many Americans. The custom of lighting candles at *brit milah* may date back to times when circumcision was performed in defiance of anti-Semitic edicts. Today, candles recall the heroism of days when burning tapers were placed in the window to signal that a *bris* was imminent and to invite friends and neighbors to the secret celebration.[52]

Since lighting Shabbat candles is a *mitzvah* that usually falls to women, candles seem particularly appropriate at ceremonies for daughters as well. Light, a symbol of the divine Presence, can be used to beautify *brit milah, brit habat,* or other ceremonies described in this book.

There is a great variety in their use. Sometimes, only one is lit for the new baby—two if there are twins. In other places, thirteen candles are customary, a reference to the number of times the word *brit* is mentioned in Genesis, with reference to *milah.*[53]

The mother and father might each light one candle, and then together light a third candle—one more for each child. (Some families add another Shabbat candle for each of their children.)

Candles may be placed anywhere in the room. A circle of light surrounding the principals makes a powerful visual statement, and the honor of lighting candles can be given to family members or friends. White Shabbat candles, braided *havdalah* candles, or a rainbow of colored candles may be used. It's up to you.

Candles can be lit in silence or with a reading, like this one.

The parents alternate lines and read the last one together:

> There is a new light in our hearts and in our home.
> These candles celebrate the birth of our child.
> Out of the creative darkness of the womb s/he has come.
> These candles celebrate her/his emergence into light.
> Blessed is the woman who bears a child, for she knows how love covers pain.
> Blessed is the man who fathers a child, for he makes a bridge between earth and heaven
> Child of light, you know not yet the love and joy overflowing from our hearts.[54]

ELIJAH'S CHAIR The decoration of the *kisei shel Eliyahu,* Elijah's chair, is a *brit milah* custom practiced by Jews worldwide. The presence of the prophet, who is associated with the coming of the Messiah, is now similarly welcomed at *brit habat* celebrations as well.

Spanish Jews drape the prophet's chair with purple and gold, and leave a prayer book or *chumash* (the book version of the Torah) on it. In other nations, Jews place a beautiful pillow or brightly colored scarves on the chair. Another option is to drape Elijah's chair with a piece of cloth that will later be made into a *tallis,* Torah binder or *wimpel.* Similarly, the baby can be brought into the room wrapped in the *wimpel* fabric. (See below.)

CLOTHING Some communities favor white clothing for the baby, others dress the baby in bright colors. The choice is yours. It is customary for baby boys to wear a little *kippah,* a *yarmulke* (skullcap), which might be the very special gift from a relative or friend who crochets. Since women in many liberal congregations wear *kippot,* this custom has been extended to *brit* ceremonies for baby girls as well.

THE WIMPEL In Eastern Europe, the cloth used to wrap an infant at his *brit milah* was later cut and sewn into a long strip for use as a Torah binder. Called a *mappah* in Hebrew, it is best known by its Yiddish name, *wimpel* (pronounced *vimpel*). In Germany and Italy, *wimpels* were lavishly decorated, painted or embroidered with the child's name, his parents' names, the date of birth, a Hebrew inscription and other decorative elements. The requirement of *hiddur mitzvah* and the absence of rabbinic law regarding *wimpels* gave rise to beautiful artifacts, many of which are displayed in Judaica collections.

The *wimpel* was presented as a family's gift to the synagogue, usually in time for use on the Shabbat closest to the child's first birthday. The Torah binder then belonged to the synagogue, and would be used when the child reached *bar mitzvah.*

The *wimpel* is enjoying a modest revival today, for daughters as well as for sons. To make a *wimpel,* simply use a beautiful piece of cotton, silk, linen, or wool as a swaddling blanket, or as

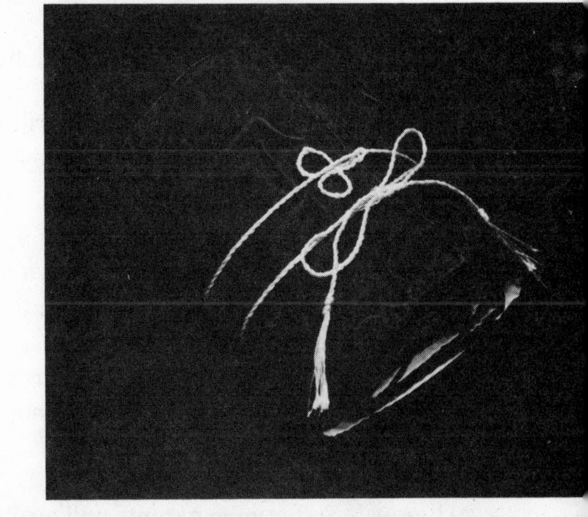

WIMPELS
(TORAH BINDINGS)

a covering for table or pillow used at the *brit.* Later, at your leisure, create a strip seven to eight inches wide and nine to twelve feet long, and decorate it as you wish, noting the child's name and birthdate.[55]

A tradition-inspired inscription might read:

> The little one, ______________, child of ______________ and ______________ was born with mazel on ______________. May God bless him/her to grow up to the study of Torah, to *huppah* and to good deeds. Amen.[56]

A quotation from the Torah portion of the week could be embroidered or written on the *wimpel,* and the design could reflect something about a child's name. The *wimpels* for boys named Aryeh often bore lions; for a daughter named Tamar, a palm tree or deer would be appropriate. In the past, the baby's zodiac sign was often featured.

Borrowing from the idea of the *wimpel,* you might use a piece of special fabric or clothing from the *brit* ceremony for later incorporation into an *atarah,* the neckpiece on a *tallit.* That prayer shawl could then be given to the child at the time of his or her *bar* or *bat mitzvah,* and perhaps even used someday as a *huppah.*

HUPPAH Sometimes parents will again raise their own marriage canopy, often a prayer shawl, to welcome the newest member of the family. Holding the poles can be an honor for special friends and family members, as it was at the wedding. The presence of older siblings under the canopy can also provide a much needed moment of recognition for older brothers and sisters who might feel lost in all the commotion surrounding the new baby.

KIDDUSH CUP *Hiddur mitzvah* applies to any object used in the ceremony. Since wine is blessed at *brit milah* and *brit habat,* a cup will be necessary—the more beautiful the better. A special cup, a gift for the baby, might be unveiled at the ceremony. Or the *kiddush* cup you used at your wedding may be filled again:

> This cup is the vessel of our hopes. We first drank from it under our wedding *huppah*. Today, it is filled with the new wine of a life just begun. In it, we taste the sweetness of the joy this child has brought us.

MUSIC

Music, song, and dance are traditional at Jewish celebrations and there are particular melodies American Jews associate with baby rituals. *Siman Tov Umazal Tov* is the all-purpose song of rejoicing, proclaiming the event as a source of joy for those gathered and for all Israel. Because of the prophet Elijah's association with *brit milah, Eliyahu Hanavi* is often sung during a bris. Since Elijah's chair is becoming a common feature of *brit habat,* it will probably become customary there as well.

Hiney Ma Tov Umanayim is another favorite at baby celebrations, since it extols the pleasure of community. *Yevarechecha Adonai Mitzion* is also popular since it includes the lines, "May you see your children's children," and "Peace be for Israel."

Additionally, there are themes, particular to families and to names, that can evoke musical responses. For example, *David* Melech Israel, and R'i *Rachel.*

When researching music for a ceremony, consult your synagogue's cantor. Even if you are not synagogue-affiliated, many cantors are glad to share their professional expertise. Ask people you know for the names of Jewish music professionals in your community.[57]

WORDS

It is customary in some circles to offer a *d'var torah,* some words of Jewish wisdom, on an occasion as important as a birth.

In addition to the weekly Torah portion, Proverbs, the Book of Psalms, and Song of Songs[58] are rich sources for such learning. Also, there is a tradition that a Psalm is given to each Jew for every year of life. Thus, if you are thirty years old, Psalm 31 is yours to enjoy, study and learn. The first Psalm is given to newborns.[59]

But nothing is more meaningful or more powerful than your own thoughts and feelings about the birth of this child; your own memories about the people for whom your baby is named. You needn't be a poet or particularly comfortable with public speaking or a Jewish scholar. If you say what is in your heart, there won't be a dry eye in the house.

Here are a few original poems of uncommon beauty, written to celebrate the birth of one special child—like yours.

A BLESSING

Berachot 17a
Eruvin 54a

May your eyes sparkle with the light of Torah,
and your ears hear the music of its words.
May the space between each letter of the scrolls
bring warmth and comfort to your soul.
May the syllables draw holiness from your heart,
and may this holiness be gentle and soothing
to you and all God's creatures.
May your study be passionate,
and meanings bear more meanings
until Life itself arrays itself before you
as a dazzling wedding feast.
And may your conversation,
even of the commonplace,
be a blessing to all who listen to your words
and see the Torah glowing on your face.

Danny Siegel
© 1985[60]

BLESSING THE CHILDREN

The mother and father place their hands on their children's heads and recite:

For the boys—

May you be as Ephraim and Menashe
of whom we know nothing
but their names
and that they were Jews.
And may you be as all Jews
whose names are lost
as witnesses to God's care,
love, and presence.
Remember them in your words,
and live Menschlich lives
as they lived Menschlich lives.

For the girls—

May you be as Sarah, Rivka, Rachel and Leah,
whose names and deeds
are our inheritance;
who bore us, raised us,
guided and taught us
that a touch
is a touch of Holiness,
and a laugh is prophecy;
that all that is ours,
is theirs;
that neither Man nor Woman alone
lights the sparks of Life,
but only both together,
generating light and warmth
and singular humanity.

Danny Siegel

BLESSING THE CHILDREN: II

May you be as Henrietta Szold,
raising and building,
that your People
need not suffer
the loneliness of pain.

May you be as Herzl and Ben Yehuda,
stung and raving with visions
for the sake of Israel
and the Jews.

And may our family be together
as Sholom Aleichem and his children,
passing on our stories to each other
with a radiance of joy
and a laugh of love.

Danny Siegel
© 1983 [62]

So you have been born, ben Sarah **
your first great birth:

from water to air
from water to land
from the mikveh/womb to the midwife's hands.

The Great-Moon-Mother-of-Miracles
brought you to birth

(from the dark, where the secret light is sown)
to sunlight!
moonlight!
candlelight!!!!!!!!

By this light, with God's aid be born
again and again
Shanah shanah

* *Son of Sarah. For a daughter, "bat Sarah."*

hodesh hodesh
hag hag
shabbat shabbat
*nes nes.**

Great-Moon-Mother-of-Miracles, multiply miracles
bless with your light the yoledet,† her child
With wave upon wave of your light, renew,
replenish your daughter,
your daughter's child.

Aviva bat Beila/slr
© 29 Heshvan 5746/1985 [63]

FOR THE NAMING OF A GIRL-CHILD

Between a boy-child and a girl-child,
only the latter has the soul's shape.
For he will grow up,
huffing and thrusting,
with a plate of armor
'round his life-breath,
and, if fortunate, will watch
this outer veil grow limber
and translucent, to reveal
his true shape with advancing age.
If not for circumcision,
he would suffocate.

But she
was husked in heaven from the start.
Her natural radiance will be
tempered by the world.
And she, more conscious of her exile,
will accept the ring someday
beneath the canopy, as if
in willful diminution of her light

* *"Year after year, month after month, holiday after holiday, sabbath after sabbath, miracle after miracle."*
† Yoledet: *a woman who has recently given birth.*

(as once, of old, the moon),
and she will take the future
in her womb, as if in trust.
And she, the nurse and blueprint
of the universe, is Israel
and the Presence quite enough,
and so the contour of the soul,
right from the first day of her life.
No sign of covenant is made in her:
she is a sign herself already,
for, waxing and waning with the moon,
she is the imprint of a world
that breathes—her own small breath
a tiny metronome by which
the world is tuned.

Joel Rosenberg
© 1987 [64]
In honor of Sara Henna Wolf Pollen's birth.

CHILD AT THE GATE OF COVENANT

So recently an expert
on the universe,
the furrow from his nose
down to his lips
drawn by an angel
at the gate of birth,
the child, ancient
as the earth, endowed
with words his mouth
can't yet pronounce,
watched by Elijah,
dabbed with wine,
a party to the covenant,
his parents stories soon
to be like ancient history:
he is gently disengaged
from pleasures of eternity,

and entered in the rolls
of life, the surge
of worldly business
like a seaswell
rolling under him,
to bear him up,
the teaching life
will soon enough
extract from him
tucked almost inaccessibly
away, behind the furrow,
deep inside.

Joel Rosenberg
© 1979 [65]
For Benjamin Yosef Novak
on the eighth day of his life,
15 Av 5739/ August 8, 1979

BRUCHA HABA'A: BLESSED SHE COMES

Welcome Woman-Child
Newborn guardian
of the sacred gift
of cycles and seasons.
Within and all around you
Be witness to the rhythms of
surrender and renewal
faith and love
Awaken intuition and knowledge
to the indwelling presence—Shechinah.

We welcome you
into the world
into your family
into your people.

May you know from your early days
how we travel through the dance
of dark and light

slavery and freedom
wandering and revelation
planting and harvest
new moon and full moon
from the illumined place of now
the sanctuary in time—Shabbat.

Hanna Tiferet Siegel
© 1985 [66]

PART FOUR

SIMCHA: JOY

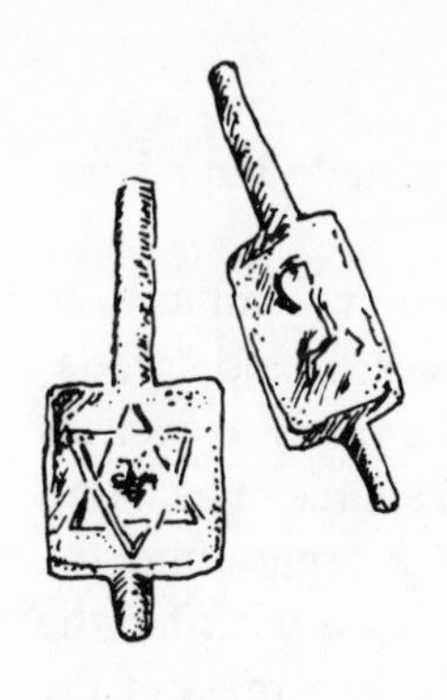

SIMCHA MEANS PARTY

The birth of a Jewish baby is always the occasion of celebration and joy. The word *simcha* means joy, and it is also the name given a joyous Jewish celebration.

If you're going to have a ceremony to welcome your new son or daughter into the covenant of Israel, you're going to have a party, a *simcha,* complete with food and drink.

Partying is not just part of Jewish culture, it is embedded in Jewish law. Indeed, *halachah* requires that all major life cycle events, like *brit milah,* include a meal called a *s'eudat mitzvah.* As *brit habat* has become a feature of Jewish observance in America, the tradition of the *s'eudat* has been extended to include it as well.*

The meals that honor the birth of a new baby range from lavish sit-down meals held in catering halls to informal buffet brunches in the family dining room. These *s'eudot mitzvot* occur in many settings and at various times of day; breakfast, after a morning *bris* at home; desserts and fruit for an Oneg Shabbat after a Friday night ceremony at the synagogue; luncheon *kiddush* after Shabbat morning *brit habat* in shul. In view of the parents'

* *Some traditional Jews prefer to call the meal following a daughter's ceremony a* s'eudat simcha, *just as they use the term* simchat bat *rather than* brit habat. *By avoiding terms associated with* mitzvot, *they avoid even the appearance of* halachic error.

state of mind and energy levels, things are usually kept fairly simple.

Foods associated with the arrival of a new child recall fertility and thus continuity: lentils, chickpeas and eggs, round "seeds" all, are part of a traditional birth *s'eudat*. The olive, as well as being round and seed-bearing, was an ancient source of heat and light, embodying the warmth and joy a baby brings into the world. Parsley, or any green vegetable, signifies a wish for the earth's continued bounty, and sweets echo the sweetness of the occasion.

Sephardic *s'eudot mitzvot* for *brit milah* include some special customs. The *seneet Elyahu hanabi,* the tray of Elijah the prophet, is a large, round, multileveled tray filled with flowers and candles, which is passed among guests, who add gifts of money. After the meal, the tray is auctioned off to the highest bidder, who distributes his bid, as well as the money on the tray, to charity.[1] And Persian Jews offer a plate of apples, a symbol of easy labor and delivery, to the young couples in attendance at the *simcha*.[2]

KASHRUT

Even for people who don't observe *kashrut,* the laws that govern what Jews eat, it is appropriate to take these regulations into account when planning for a meal after a *brit*. Observing *kashrut* will avoid embarrassment, discomfort, and hunger for observant relatives and friends. Also, a *mohel,* cantor, or rabbi who officiates at your ceremony may not be able to partake of the feast if you do not observe the conventions. Generally, if the party is to take place in a synagogue, you will be required to observe the dietary laws.

Kashrut is best understood not as an ancient health code but as a way of sanctifying the basic human need for food. The laws are based on specific proscriptions in the Bible, for example, against eating birds of prey and fish lacking fins and scales. The separation of milk and meat is an elaboration on the Torah's command not to "boil a kid in its mother's milk."

Briefly, *kashrut* permits the following foods: all vegetables and fruits, fish with fins and scales (no shellfish or bottom-feeding fish), domestic fowl, and animals that both chew a cud and have split hooves. For meat to be kosher, the animal must also be killed according to specific ritual laws by someone who recites a blessing, and then the meat must be soaked and salted to remove all traces of blood. Finally, meat and milk products are not eaten at the same meal and must be kept separate. Thus, *milchig* (dairy) and *flayshig* (meat) foods are not cooked in the same pots or served on the same dishes. The customary waiting period between consumption of meat and milk varies according to custom, from one to six hours.

To find a kosher caterer, ask for recommendations from friends, family, or your rabbi. Failing that, consult the Yellow Pages under "Catering." In larger cities and towns, there is usually a special listing of kosher services. "Kosher style" means the restaurant or caterer specializes in Jewish-identified foods, such as knishes and lox, but it is usually a signal that the food is not really kosher.

GETTING ORGANIZED

There are people who bake and freeze all the goodies for the *simcha* well in advance. For parents and grandmothers-to-be who enjoy baking, this can provide a very useful outlet for the nervous energy that comes with waiting. Likewise, if you plan to have a catered meal, you might want to contact a caterer and make menu selections in advance. If you find yourself with time to spare before the baby comes, it's a good idea to compile a guest list for your *simcha,* complete with phone numbers.

In the best of all possible worlds, new parents are not the ones who organize and host a *s'eudat mitzvah.* In Sephardic communities, paying for the food and drink at a *brit* is considered an honor assumed by the *sandek.* Similarly, the cost of the *s'eudat* is often the very joyful gift of grandparents.

Close friends and relatives may offer to bring food to the *s'eudat mitzvah;* this can add a very *haimish,* or homey, touch to the gathering. But if you really prefer to do it yourself or let a caterer take care of everything, ask the folks who offer for a raincheck in the form of a covered-dish meal, to be delivered during the first weeks at home with the new baby.

In any event, remember that your guests are coming to share your joy and see the baby—not to be entertained by you.

CELEBRATING

Before beginning the meal, a nice way to honor a special guest is to ask them to say the *motzi,* the blessing over bread, traditionally made over a large braided loaf of challah.

If your *brit* ceremony did not include time for guests to offer their blessings and wishes for the baby and family, the meal offers an opportunity for doing this. If telegrams or messages have come from afar, these might be read aloud. During or after eating, *divrei Torah,* words of Torah or learning, might be delivered, about the baby's name, about the date of his or her birth, about the Jewish context into which this child has been born. Some guests might be asked in advance to think about what they might like to say. A designated "master of ceremonies" (some uncle or sister who has a snappy comeback for every occasion) can turn this time into a memorable party.

If there was no appropriate time for an older sibling to participate during the *brit* ceremony, the baby's brother(s) or sister(s) might be given a chance to shine for a moment during the meal. If the children are old enough, they could compose a few words of welcome for the new baby. On a day he or she is feeling more than a little eclipsed by the new baby, holding the center of attention for a few minutes can be important.

The traditional ending for a *s'eudat mitzvah* is the singing of the *birkat hamazon,* the blessings after eating. There is a special *birkat* for the meal following a *bris* that includes blessings for the baby, parents, *mohel,* and *sandek.*[3] It is an honor to be asked to lead the company in these prayers, called *benching,* and it is customary to distribute copies of the *birkat hamazon* to the guests. Some parents include these prayers in Xeroxed sheets or booklets they prepare for guests at the *brit.*

BOOKLETS

It is becoming increasingly common to provide a printed guide or booklet to accompany your *brit,* or any of the other ceremonies mentioned in this book. The explanations, translations, responsive readings, poems or prayers you provide, can help your guests feel informed and involved. And the booklet will become a family treasure.

Booklets for your celebration can be simple or elaborate, a single Xeroxed sheet or a pamphlet of many pages. Sometimes, the cover is a copy of the birth announcement. It can be a program of the entire ceremony, or it can simply provide information about the baby's name or explanations of customs you have incorporated, such as giving *tsedakah* in honor of the birth.

However, many families do not have the energy or time for such a project. The absence of a booklet does not necessarily detract from the ceremony. In fact, some rabbis feel that a "libretto" can dampen the spontaneity of the event.

PHOTOGRAPHY

In just a few years, all records of his or her babyhood will become a source of fascination to your child, so make sure there are film and flash on hand.

Some parents, *mohels,* and rabbis object to the presence of cameras during *brit* ceremonies, especially the *milah* or circumcision part of a *bris.* Others welcome as much photography—video or still—as possible. A tape recorder is always an unobtrusive way to capture the spirit of the day.

A *s'eudat mitzvah* is always an opportunity for picture-taking. In general, people don't hire professional photographers for so intimate a celebration. Ask a relative or friend who is good with a camera to do the honors. And while candid pictures are wonderful, posed shots of proud grandparents holding the baby, and photographs of every conceivable family grouping, will become treasured keepsakes as time passes.

GIFTS

Jewish baby gifts range from the silly (bibs that feature cute Yiddish phrases like *Bubbe's Fresser*—Grandma's big eater) to the sublime (heirlooms, like Grandpa's engraved *kiddush* cup). Adding a Jewish dimension to gift giving means seeking out records or tapes of Israeli children's songs, and children's books with Jewish content. For the newborn protoreader, there are cloth, plastic, and cardboard books that feature the Hebrew alphabet. A baby blanket with *Layla Tov* (good night) woven into the design is available.[4] And there's nothing wrong with funny bibs.

Decorative pieces suitable for hanging in the nursery are a new form of distinctively Jewish baby gifts. These range from bright posters of the *aleph-bet* to hand-lettered works of art.

Calligraphers around the country are creating beautiful, personalized works that both delight the eye and commemorate the arrival of a new Jew. Some of these take the form of a kind of birth certificate, including the Hebrew date and/or the name of the weekly *parasha* (Torah reading), as well as the name of the baby and parents in Hebrew and English. Some calligraphers draw and illuminate the baby's name in Hebrew, or in both Hebrew and English. Sometimes, elements of the *brit* ceremony are featured.

There are calligraphic acrostic "poems," using the letters of the name to begin lines from the Torah. Family trees have inspired some wonderful pieces of art. It all depends on the imagination of the gift giver and the skill of the artist.

Certain gifts become heirlooms from the moment they are given. A *tallis* given by grandparents to a grandson becomes a tangible link that may recall their relationship to generations unimagined. Other objects in this category might include a charity box, or a colorful *mezuzah* case that could follow the new baby from her nursery, to her girlhood room, into her first home as an adult, and perhaps even onto the doorposts of her own baby's room. In some families, a handcrafted silver or brass *dreydl* has replaced the proverbial silver spoon as a special gift.

Handmade gifts are always very special. People who work in needlepoint have created hangings based on a baby's name, or made a cross-stitch *aleph-bet* for the nursery. People who work with wood fashion wooden blocks with a baby's name painted in Hebrew and English on them. One woman appliqués the letters of the baby's Hebrew name on soft fabric cubes, an idea that deserves application to a baby quilt as well. Even something as small and simple as a hand-crocheted *kippah* for a baby boy to wear during the *bris* is a gift beyond price.

According to tradition, trees were planted at the birth of a child: a cypress sapling for a girl, a cedar for a boy. Later, two branches from each would be cut for the wedding canopy. Today, family and friends commonly mark the child's birth by having a tree planted in Israel.

©Rose Ann Chasman

Blessing for a Daughter

Amulet

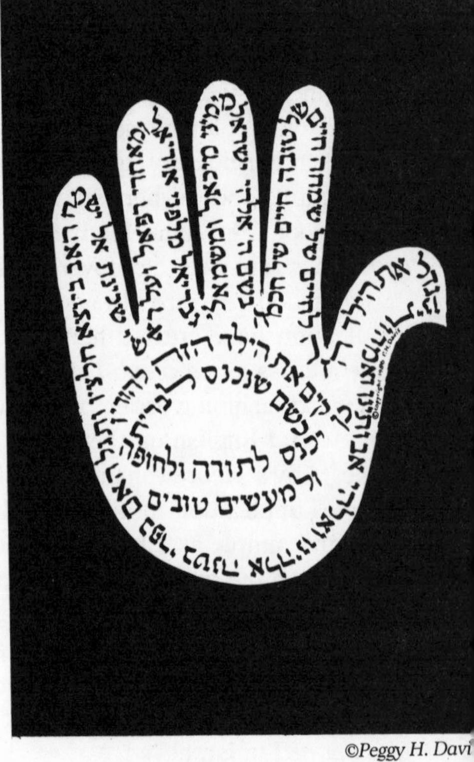

©Peggy H. Davi

BABY-NAMING CERTIFICATE

אלוהינו ואלוהי אבותינו ואמותינו,
קיים את הילד הזה לאביו ולאמו
ויקרא שמו בישראל
כשם שנכנס לברית כן יכנס לתורה ולחופה ולמעשים טובים
נולד ביום לחודש שנת תש

Our God and God of our ancestors, sustain this child for mother and father
and let name be called in Israel

Just as you are now entering the covenant, so too may you come to acquire Torah,
establish a home of your own and do rightly. Born on

I WILL BLESS YOU, AND YOUR DESCENDANTS WILL BE AS NUMEROUS AS THE STARS OF THE SKY AND THE SAND UPON THE SEA SHORE.
GENESIS 22:17

To do this, send a check for $5.00 for each tree to the Jewish National Fund, 42 East 69th Street, New York NY 10021. If you like, specify that you wish the tree planted in the Children's Forest and include the name and address of the child in whose honor the tree is given, as well as the name and address of the donor. An attractive announcement of the gift is then mailed to the baby's family. For more information, call 212-879-9300 or 212-737-7441.

Finally, thoughtful guests will bring a little gift to the baby's older sibling(s) who invariably feel very left out on such occasions. It does not have to be a big present—just a token to help older kids know that they are remembered and loved.

CELEBRATIONS AND CUSTOMS

There are a number of lesser-known Jewish ceremonies and customs that commemorate the arrival of baby. Some of these, like donations of charity and linking a *brit* celebration to the plight of Soviet Jews, are as pressing and current as the day's headlines. Others are unknown to American Jews and may seem quaint. All of them, however, share the sense that a birth is proper cause for a community celebration.

TSEDAKAH

Traditionally, Jews mark happy occasions like births, weddings, and *b'nai mitzvah,* with contributions of *tsedakah,* righteous giving or charity. This is a way of both sharing the joy of the occasion and of acknowledging that personal happiness is incomplete in a world so badly in need of repair. A donation made to honor the birth of a child is an investment in the more just world we all wish for our children. It is also an example for children to emulate.

Although it is customary to give to Jewish organizations, donations may be made to any agency or program you consider worthy. It is common to give some multiple of $18 because the numerical value for eighteen is spelled out with the Hebrew letters for the word life—*chai.* Among Sephardim, the number twenty-six, the numerical equivalent of God's name, is the base for giving.

Although tradition declares *tsedakah* is best when it is given anonymously, a simple announcement of your gift, made either during a ceremony or in an accompanying booklet, may encourage others to make a contribution on this or a similar occasion. And that would be a *mitzvah.*

Two relatively new, unique avenues for this form of personal *tsedakah* are:

Mazon, a Jewish Response to Hunger, an effort to share celebratory meals of all sorts with the world's hungry. Mazon channels contributions to various feeding programs in the United States and around the world. With voluntary donations of 3 percent of the food costs of a *simcha,* synagogues and individuals can acknowledge their connection to people who lack the means to feed their children.

For information or to contribute, contact Mazon, 2940 Westwood Boulevard, Suite #7, Los Angeles CA 90064, (213) 470-7769.

Ziv Tzedakah Fund, a nonprofit organization that collects and distributes funds to various little-known grassroots projects in Israel and the United States. The lifework of Danny Siegel, poet and *tzedakah* teacher, Ziv ("radiance") provides money and support for individuals and programs providing direct services to the needy. Ziv has supported an Israeli woman who cares for children with Down's Syndrome; a Philadelphia teeenager who single-handedly began a campaign to help homeless people; a synagogue shelter in North Carolina. Ziv is also involved in bringing the message of *tsedakah* to communities and schools throughout the United States, Canada, and Israel.

For information or to contribute, contact Ziv Tzedakah Fund, c/o Bena Siegel, treasurer, 11818 Trail Ridge Drive, Potomac MD 20854.

TWINNING

The idea of twinning or linking a life-cycle event between an American Jew and a Soviet refusenik is most often associated with *bar* and *bat mitzvah* ceremonies. However, some families have chosen to bring this custom to their *brit milah* and *brit habat* observances. By speaking the name and pain of the Russian child and family who cannot freely practice their Judaism, American Jews affirm their solidarity with them.

"Twinning" a ceremony can be accomplished very simply. It is enough to repeat a blessing using the name of the refusenik baby, or to recite the benedictions that include the naming. Parents often make some statement about their reasons for twinning the ceremony and many make a donation to an organization working for the release of Soviet Jews. To find the name of a Soviet family that would be appropriate, contact a local organization or agency working for the release and resettlement of Russian Jews.[5]

PIDYON HABEN

While every baby is cherished, the birth of a first child is an unparalleled experience; the potential for life has been fulfilled and the world will never be the same. It seems appropriate that there should be a Jewish acknowledgment of the momentous passage from adulthood to parenthood.

Pidyon haben, the redemption of the firstborn son, is one of the oldest of all Jewish rituals, mentioned in the book of Exodus. In America, however, many Jews have abandoned it altogether or observe it only perfunctorily. For many, the ceremony seemed hopelessly legalistic, empty of spirit or celebration. But the current revival of interest in traditional ritual has focused attention on *pidyon haben,* a ceremony that speaks to the powerful feelings evoked by your firstborn.

In many ancient cultures, the firstborn child, especially sons, enjoyed a special—if not always salutary—status. There are many interpretations for the alleged practice of sacrificing firstborns; the custom has been ascribed to the unconscious desire to kill off a usurping son. But firstborns also evoke a more generalized sense that the life force of the universe requires some token of appeasement, or at least thanks, for the audaciousness of procreation.

Biblical society shared that belief in the specialness of a firstborn son. Seen in this light, the tenth plague visited upon the Egyptians in the story of Exodus—the killing of all firstborn sons—was a truly unspeakable punishment. And it was their exemption on that terrible night that obligated all firstborn Jewish sons to serve God—specifically, as members of a priesthood that lived apart from their families, in the service of the Temple.

Even when the obligation of priestly service became limited to Levites and their descendants, firstborn sons were not exempt from a ritual release, or redemption, from the obligation set forth in the Torah.

The redemption was accomplished by asking a *kohane,* a priest or descendant of priests, to accept five shekels in exchange for the son's obligation. According to *halachah, pidyon haben* must take place on the thirty-first day after birth.[6] If that should fall on Shabbat or a holiday, however, the ceremony is postponed until the following day.

The status of "firstborn" depends entirely upon the mother. *Pidyon haben* is only required if a baby boy quite literally opens his mother's womb. Thus, if a woman has given birth to a girl, if she has miscarried, or even if she gave birth by cesarean section, the ceremony is not performed. Nor is the ceremony required for firstborn sons whose fathers are either *kohane* or *levi,* or whose mother is the daughter of a *kohane* or *levi* father.

The father is charged with performing the *mitzvah,* though if he cannot or does not discharge his obligation, the community may act for him. If a firstborn is not redeemed as a child, he may take the obligation upon himself when he comes of age.

In some communities, the baby would be presented to a *kohane*[7] on an ornate metal-work plate, and a special token took the place of the coins. The plate would be a community possession, the property of the synagogue, while the token was given to the family. In America, it became customary to use five silver dollars in place of five shekels, and rabbis often took over the priestly function.

Pidyon haben is very brief, consisting of a few exchanges between the father and the *kohane*.[8] The father presents the baby and offers money as a substitute for giving up his son. The *kohane* accepts the offer, announces the substitution, pronounces the threefold priestly blessing, and the company proceeds to eat, drink and be merry.

TRADITIONAL PIDYON HABEN

FATHER: *(Presenting the child to the* kohane*)* This is my firstborn, and the firstborn of his mother's womb. The Holy One, blessed be the One, has commanded us to redeem him, as it is written in the Torah, "At the age of one month shall you redeem him for five shekels." And it is written, "Sanctify unto Me the firstborn of the children of Israel—for they are Mine."

KOHANE: Which do you prefer? Give me your firstborn son, the firstborn of his mother, or redeem him for five shekels, as it is written in the Torah?

FATHER: I choose to redeem him and here is his redemption money, as prescribed by the Torah.

The *kohane* takes the money and returns the child to his father, who says:

בָּרוּךְ אַתָּה יְיָ, אֱלֹהֵינוּ מֶלֶךְ הָעוֹלָם אֲשֶׁר קִדְּשָׁנוּ בְּמִצְוֹתָיו, וְצִוָּנוּ עַל פִּדְיוֹן הַבֵּן.

Praised are You, Ruler of the Universe, who has sanctified us with your commandments concerning the redemption of the firstborn.

Parents recite the *shehehiyanu.*

KOHANE: *(Holding the redemption money over the child's head)* This is instead of that; this is in exchange for that. May this child now enter upon a life of Torah and awe of heaven. May it be God's will that as he has attained redemption, that he be led to Torah, the *huppah* and good deeds. Amen.

May God make you like Ephraim and Menashe.

He recites the priestly benediction.

The kohane, rabbi or an honored guest recites kiddush, and a meal is served.

NEW FORMS Recently *pidyon haben* has been the inspiration and foundation for new ceremonies. Called by various names, *pidyon habat* (redemption of the firstborn daughter) or *kiddush petter rechem* (sanctification of the one who opens the womb),[9] or *seder kedushat chaye hamishpachah* (ceremony of consecration to family life),[10] they all share certain elements.

The emphasis in new *pidyon* ceremonies is on the unique experience of a first child, and on the parents' dedication to the continuity of the Jewish people. The new rituals are inclusive of all firstborn children, girls as well as boys, children born by cesarean section, or after a miscarriage. The focus is not on redeeming a child from obligations, but on sanctifying and dedicating the child for a life of service. The Passover story is recalled, connecting the beginning of parenthood and the birth of the Jewish people.

Certain ritual elements of traditional *pidyon haben* are maintained, linking new ceremonies to the ancient one. Among these are the presentation of the child to the rabbi or *mesader,* "the one who orders" the ceremony; a dialogue between the rabbi and parents that includes an exchange of coins, now usually given to a Jewish charity and representing the child's first contribution to the community; and, of course, celebration.

Since few people are familiar with the ritual, parents often distribute a booklet or broadsheet explaining the ceremony and its significance.

A NEW CEREMONY FOR PIDYON[11]

This is our son/daughter, our first-born, who opened the womb of his/her mother. As it is written: Consecrate to Me all the firstborn; whatever is the first to open the womb among the people of Israel. (Exodus 13:2)

Having been privileged to realize the fulfillment of the potential for life within us, may our sense of reverence for the sanctity of all life be awakened.

חָבִיב אָדָם שֶׁנִּבְרָא בְּצֶלֶם חִבָּה יְתֵרָה נוֹדַעַת לוֹ שֶׁנִּבְרָא בְּצֶלֶם שֶׁנֶּאֱמַר כִּי בְּצֶלֶם אֱלֹהִים עָשָׂה אֶת הָאָדָם (פרקי אבות ג:יח).
בָּרוּךְ אַתָּה יְיָ זוֹכֵר יְצוּרָיו לְחַיִּים בְּרַחֲמִים.

Beloved are men and women for they are created in the image of God. It is a sign of special love that we are aware of the moral responsibility this places upon us.

Blessed be the Presence Whose sanctity fills creation that in love remembers us for life.

The consecration of the firstborn also serves as a recollection of the Exodus from Egypt.

וְהָיָה כִּי־יִשְׁאָלְךָ בִנְךָ מָחָר לֵאמֹר מַה־זֹּאת וְאָמַרְתָּ אֵלָיו בְּחֹזֶק יָד הוֹצִיאָנוּ יְיָ מִמִּצְרַיִם מִבֵּית עֲבָדִים.

It is written: And when in time to come your child asks you, "What does this mean?" you shall say, "By strength of hand the Eternal brought us out of Egypt, from the house of bondage." (Exodus 13-14)

The experience of the Exodus from Egyptian bondage has ever sensitized our people to the values of human freedom and dignity. May we exemplify these values as we grow together as a family, creating a home where love of Torah, awareness of that which is Godly, and compassion for humanity always abide; where the hearts of the parents and the hearts of the children shall always be turned to one another.

Representative of the community:

Blessed with the sacred trust of new life, will you dedicate yourselves to the redeeming of life?

Parents:

We desire that the birth of our son/daughter inspire us to work for the redemption of all life. We express our partnership with that which is Godly in the process of *tikun olam,* world redemption, as we, in honor of the birth of our child ____________ bat/ben ____________ v' ____________, present a gift of *tsedakah.* May it be a symbol of our and his/her commitment to Torah, to involvement in the life of our people, and to the upholding of those values which make for human dignity, fellowship, and peace.

Blessed by the Presence Whose sanctity fills our lives, we redeem every first born and engage in *tikun olam.*

Parents present a gift of *tsedakah.*

זֶה תַּחַת זֶה, זֶה חָלוּף זֶה, זֶה מָחוּל עַל זֶה

This *tsedakah* instead of greed
This gift in place of selfishness
This commitment because of the blessing of new life.

Rabbi:

וְיִכָּנֵס זֶה הַבֵּן (וְתִכָּנֵס זֹאת הַבַּת) לְחַיִּים, לְתוֹרָה וּלְיִרְאַת שָׁמַיִם. יְהִי רָצוֹן
שֶׁכְּשֵׁם שֶׁנִּכְנַס (שֶׁנִּכְנְסָה) לַבְּרִית, כֵּן יִכָּנֵס (תִּכָּנֵס) לְתוֹרָה וּלְחֻפָּה וּלְמַעֲשִׂים טוֹבִים.

Parents:

May our son/daughter enter into life, Torah and a commitment to all that is Godly. As he/she has entered into the covenant, may he/she grow into a life of Torah, *huppah* and good deeds.

Parents recite the *shehehiyanu.*

All present recite *kiddush* and *motzi,* the blessing over bread, which is dipped in honey.

The rabbi recites the priestly benediction.

FIRST DAYS

In the past, the first days of a child's life, especially of a son, were marked by ritual visits to the family's home by relatives, friends, and neighbors. Some of these customs are still observed in Hasidic and Orthodox communities, but for most American Jews, whose families tend to be scattered around the country and who place a high value on privacy, they may seem intrusive or invasive. However, in recalling a time when an entire community celebrated each new life, these customs offer liberal Jews models for communal celebration and observance.

Shalom Zachar, welcome to the male, or son, was celebrated on the first Friday night after the birth of a son. If the baby was born on a Friday evening after Shabbat candles had been lit, people would arrive, unannounced but expected, that very night.

Guests assembled in the new baby's home to recite psalms, sing songs, and discuss Torah. Little children were invited to recite the *shema* near the cradle and adult visitors offered prayers on behalf of the new arrival and his mother, attuning the baby's ears to the sound of Hebrew from his first days on earth.

In addition to gifts of food, charms and amulets would be brought to the home as a way of banishing the evil spirits, especially Lilith, who was supposedly attracted to newborns in the especially vulnerable period before *brit milah* and naming.

Legend has it that, while in the womb, babies learn the entire Torah, but just before birth an angel causes the infant to forget all he knows. *Shalom Zachar* was an opportunity to console him for this loss.[12]

In our day, it is quite likely that the first Shabbat of a baby's life will be spent in the hospital and even if the baby is home, the family may prefer its privacy to a house full of guests. But *Shalom Zachar* can turn a steady stream of unacquainted visitors into a community. For families who feel ready to handle a more concentrated expression of welcome, a *Shalom Zachar* or a *Shalom Nekavah,* welcome to the daughter, can be organized by a relative or friends as an hour-long coffee-and-dessert event. A blessing over wine, a *shehehiyanu,* a chorus of *Siman Tov Umazel Tov* and voilà!

There are special circumstances where *Shalom Zachar/Nekavah* can provide a very nice model for welcoming a child. When a baby or child has been adopted, or for the baby brought home from the hospital after a stay necessitated by medical complications, the first Shabbat evening at home might be an appropriate time for a gathering. Something as simple as shared meal provided by thoughtful friends, song, candlelight, and loving support makes an auspicious beginning and a cherished memory.

Another celebration held the night before a *bris* was called *Vach Nacht,* watch night, or *Lel Shemurim,* the night of the vigil. Newborn sons and their mothers would not be left alone for an instant on this night, when they were perceived to be in mortal danger from Lilith and other demons. In order to protect the little one, a mixture of magic and piety was employed; a *minyan* of praying men surrounded mother and child invoking God's blessing, and a chalk circle on the floor kept out the demons.

Sephardic Jews celebrate a similar custom called *Zocher HaBrit,* "remembering the *brit,*" but without the preoccupation with demons and darkness. In some communities, the night before a *bris* is celebrated with a festive meal in the grandfather's home, complete with dancing and singing. Elsewhere, the celebration is held at the home of the *sandek* and then moves in a torchlit, singing procession to the home of the new baby.[13]

Modern parents who view the *mitzvah* of *brit milah* with some trepidation report that the presence of sympathetic friends the night before the circumcision is a great comfort. Most helpful is the testimony and support of other parents who felt similar anxiety and lived through the event. This is especially true if the impending *bris* is for an older, adopted child for whom the procedure may be more complex. Meditation and prayer, or just hand-holding, can help parents get through a trying time.

Hollekreish, another Eastern European custom, was probably borrowed from Christian neighbors and based on ancient pagan custom. The original meaning of *Hollekreish* is obscure. *Kreish* comes from the German for scream or shriek. And while some rabbis prefer to trace *Holle* to the Hebrew *chol* (profane or secular), more likely it refers to an ancient Teutonic goddess Holle or Holda, who played the part of Lilith in the pantheon of German mythology. *Hollekreish* was probably meant to scare the demon Holle away from a baby and mother until baptism would protect them.[14]

Customs varied from one town to the next. In some communities, *Hollekreish* was celebrated only for boys, and elsewhere the practice included girls.[15] The children of the community would be invited to the new baby's home on the fourth Shabbat of his or her life. They would assemble around the baby's cradle; if the baby was a girl, the female children would be given the greater honors; for a boy, the male children would be featured.

The father, cantor, or the children themselves would read selected biblical verses. Then the crib would be lifted into the air three times and each time the father would ask:

Hollekreish, hollekreish;
wie soll das kindchen heissen.
(What should the little child be called?)

The children would shout the baby's secular name each time, and be rewarded for their efforts with sweets.

YOLEDET

A *yoledet* is a woman who has recently given birth. The term is based on the Hebrew word for giving birth. Yemenite Jews have traditional ceremonies that honor the *yoledet,* accompanied by music and festive foods. While the recorded customs of Ashkenazic Jews refer only to men, a gathering of women around a mother before her son's circumcision seems so natural, that it was doubtless an undocumented gathering/observance for our Eastern European great-grandmothers as well.

The special status of the new mother has been given special attention in American Jewish circles recently, by intimate *rosh hodesh* groups, small gatherings of women who meet to observe the new moon.[16] The poem that appears on page 180 was written for a Boston area *rosh hodesh* group's celebration for two of its newly delivered members.

American celebrations for the *yoledet,* focusing on the momentous changes in the new mother's life, are only just beginning. If you deferred having a baby shower, a party with gifts, songs, sweets and the company of loving female family and friends can become a celebration for you in your new role as *yoledet.*

TREE PLANTING

As previously mentioned, it was customary in ancient Israel to plant a cedar sapling at the birth of a boy, a cypress when a baby girl was born. The cedar symbolized strength and stature; the cypress gentleness and sweetness. The children were expected to care for the trees planted in their honor, and eventually branches were cut down for use in their *huppah*.

Today, it is customary to plant a tree in Israel to honor the birth of a child. (See pages 193–196.) However, planting a tree in your own backyard when a baby is born is a delightful thing to do, something parents might do alone, or incorporate into many of the celebrations described in this book.

With a few words of explanation, a *shehehiyanu* and a festive meal, the planting of a tree might be its own celebration, timed to commemorate the milestone of your choice: the first tooth, the first word, the first birthday.

THE EVIL EYE

Many Jewish customs were prompted by fear of the evil eye and of dark and malicious spirits. In some communities, packets of almonds, nuts and sweets were attached to the cradle to keep the spirits occupied. Red ribbons were tied around the crib. Biblical verses were posted around the baby's room.[17]

The pervasive dread of the *ayn horeh,* evil eye, necessitated an etiquette about what you could or could not say about a new baby. For fear of attracting the jealousy of the demon world, one would never extol the beauty of a baby, at least not without mentioning some "flaw," spitting three times, or at least saying, *kayn aynhoreh*.

As quaint as these beliefs may seem, the unspoken awe and fear that surrounds the mystery of birth is still with us. Many

Jews will not buy a layette, will not have a crib in the house, and will not allow a baby shower before a baby is born. When asked, we claim that our reticence is based on concern that something might, God forbid, happen to the baby and then it would be too painful to have all that paraphernalia around. But then, even thinking such a thought requires that you spit three times to dispel the evil eye. Old superstitions die hard.

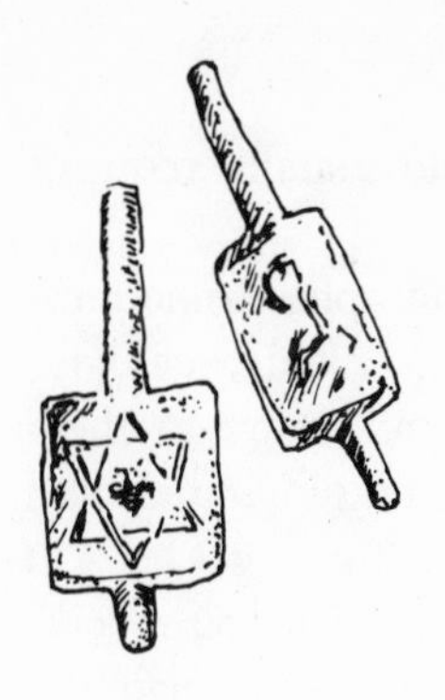

ANNOUNCEMENTS

A birth announcement shares your joy with others. And while the printed card is a time-honored American custom, in recent years there has been a trend toward creating announcements that celebrate the fact that a *Jewish* baby has been born.

In general, birth announcements tend to be simpler than wedding announcements, mostly because you want to get the news out as quickly as possible. They are usually sent out within a month of the baby's arrival. However, not everyone is able to meet that sort of deadline and it really makes no difference when your cards go out; people are delighted to get the news whenever it arrives.

The creative possibilities are endless. Your news can be printed inside pink or blue cards from a stationery shop; or you can write a personal note inside art cards from a museum, gallery or Judaica store. You can illustrate your own announcements, or have a friend design it as a very special baby gift. Many professional printers offer Hebrew lettering and do-it-yourselfers can find press-apply Hebrew letters at most Judaica shops.

Computer produced announcements have become quite sophisticated graphically, and can showcase your Hebrew software. At the other end of the spectrum, thermography, which produces the handsome raised type associated with engraving, makes for a very striking announcement and usually requires some advance planning.

One increasingly popular option is the calligraphed announcement, examples of which appear in this book. Talented calligraphers now work in most American cities and many of them advertise in Jewish newspapers. If your wedding invitation was the work of a calligrapher, this is a wonderful time to get back in touch with him or her for another assignment. Or if you receive a striking birth announcement, ask the parents for the name of the artist. If you don't know where to begin looking for a calligrapher, your rabbi may be able to recommend someone. (A list of calligraphers appears on page 251.)

If you opt for a calligrapher, it is helpful to meet with the artist in advance of the baby's birth. Some couples who know the sex and have selected the child's name commission the announcement in advance and simply call in relevant details once the baby is born. Others select a design and give the artist the boy's and girl's names they have selected, and phone the calligrapher from the hospital with the news.

The Hebrew *aleph-bet* has long inspired beautiful calligraphy so that the baby's name can be its own ornament. Artists can design announcements to feature those elegant letters in distinctive ways; the use of a family tree, for example, makes for a very special statement. The branching pairs of names leading to this tiny newcomer are more than design elements, more than family history even; they present a map of the continuity of the Jewish people in one family.

And when a Hebrew name happens to refer to an animal or plant, a drawing can add a charming element; one calligrapher adds a teddy bear for babies named Dov, the Hebrew for bear.[18]

WHAT TO SAY

There are no rules about what you can or cannot, should or should not say on a birth announcement. Etiquette and tradition suggest nothing but the baby's name, the parents' names, date of birth, weight and length. Few people have varied from the bare-bones announcement, so the addition of a quotation or personal message always makes for something special.

Even if you know little or no Hebrew, the presence of Hebrew on the announcement marks it as Jewish. The simple addition of the baby's Hebrew name in Hebrew letters can suffice. Another easy way to add a Jewish element is to give the birthdate in both Gregorian and lunar Jewish dates: "January 26, 1985 / 5 Shevat 5745." You might also want to tell people if yours was a Shabbat baby, or if she was born during a holiday, or on *rosh hodesh,* the new moon.

The text of one announcement reads:

Hannah Yael enunciated her arrival
on the third day of Hannukah.
27 Kislev 5746—10 December 1985

Ellie Jonathan & Aviva Kremer

A card that reads something like "Oren Michael has joined our family," signed by "Joan Klein, Raphael Stein, and Zachary Stein," helps make big sisters and brothers feel important. It also acknowledges that the entire family has grown and changed with the addition of a new member.

Some parents now include mention of the person or people in whose honor the baby was named on the announcement:

Karen Appel and Mark Fine
joyfully announce the birth of their daughter
Abigail Appel Fine
May 25, 1984 23 Iyar 5744
Named after paternal grandfather Abraham Fine

Another announcement simply included the line "Ruth Doviva is named after Marty's grandmother Rivka and Esther's grandfather Dov."

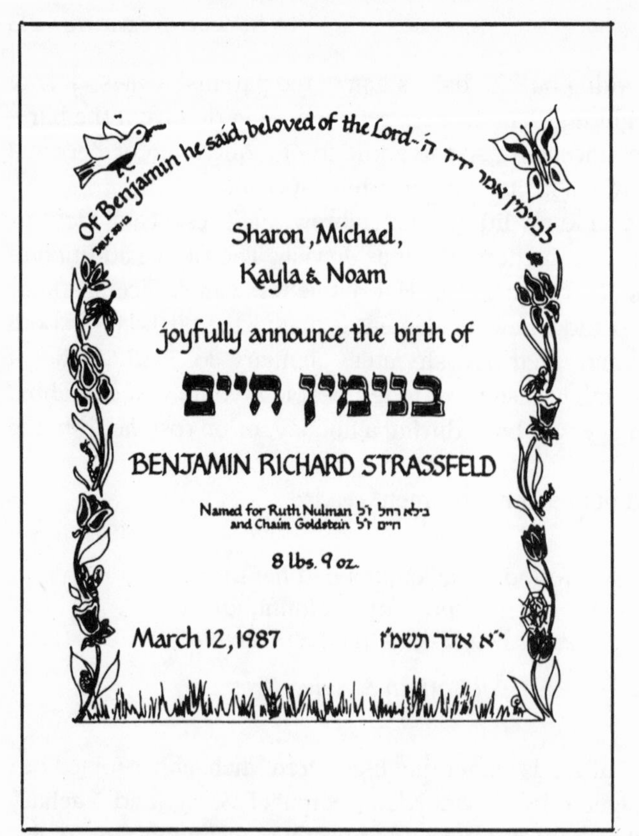

©Betsy Platkin Teutsch

©Susan Leviton

OPPOSITE,
TWO BIRTH ANNOUNCEMENTS

BIRTH ANNOUNCEMENT, COVER AND FAMILY TREE

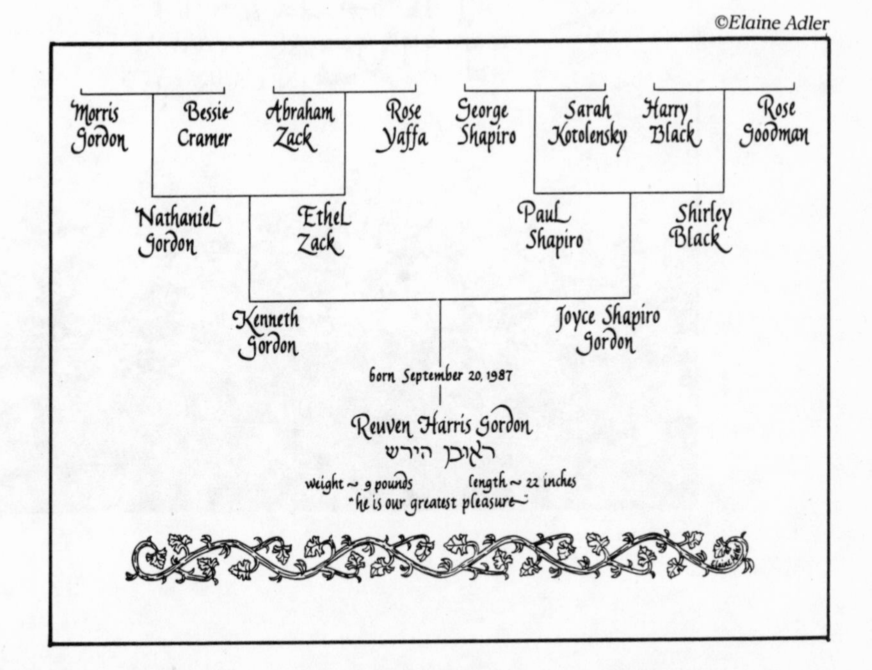

Birth announcement, cover and text

While it has become customary to include the baby's weight and length at birth on the announcement, some parents have omitted this information in favor of more personal and evocative details. For example:

Leora was born with a full head of soft, dark hair.

When Levi was born, he did not cry, but opened his eyes and looked around the room until he seemed to find our faces.

Avi has the long fingers and toes of his father's family, and shares the gift of healthy, lusty lungs with his big brother Adam.

Mimi is a good eater, and thank God, a good sleeper!

Many beautiful additions to Jewish announcements come from the Bible. Some amplify the joy of the occasion, some have to do with the baby's name. On their announcement of Solomon's birth, his parents included the line: "David comforted his wife Bat Sheva . . . and she bore a son. He was called *Solomon* and the Lord loved him." For a Debra, there is "Awake Deborah and sing." To find a biblical quotation that includes your baby's name, check a biblical concordance or ask your rabbi or cantor.

Meaningful quotes can come from the Torah portion of the week in which your baby was born. Or look for lines of poetry in Psalms or the Song of Songs, the daily prayer book or from other traditional or modern Jewish books with which you are familiar. There are quotations throughout this book that are suitable for use in a birth announcement, especially in the chapters on *Brit Milah, Brit Habat, Hiddur Mitzvah:* Beautiful Touches, and Adoption. A few examples follow here:

Light shine upon us
Our people have increased
And our joy is made great

For we have born a child
May there be no end of peace.

from Isaiah 9

With each child, the world begins anew.

Midrash

By the breath of children God sustains the world.

Shabbat 119b

Today is the birthday of the world.

Rosh Hashana Liturgy

(especially for a child born around the new year)

This little child, may he (she) grow big.

(from the daily prayerbook)

THE ADOPTED BABY

Adoption announcements bring the same good news as birth announcements—a new member of the family has arrived, a new member of the Jewish people is here. All the suggestions and quotations above apply to the announcement of an adoption. By including the name or names of those in whose honor the child is named, you help people understand how this "graft" on your family tree is no less integral to its life than biological children.

Adoption announcements sometimes give two "birth" dates for the child. One tells the date of the child's birth and, especially in the case of an international adoption, the nation. The other date announces when the child was born as a member of your family:

Alexander Micah
Born: December 12, 1986 in Bogota, Colombia
Arrived home: February 18, 1987

Parents choose different ways of dealing with names that were given to their children prior to adoption. Some announce a change of name, others the addition of a new one. For example:

Our daughter is home!
Rachel Susan Feldman-Bright
born
Seong Ae Han
(Beauty and Sincerity)

or

Welcome
Nina Seong Mee Park (Beautiful Star) Gruber

This poem about the special gift of an adopted baby is often included or excerpted in adoption announcements and in adoption ceremonies:

We did not plant you,
True.
But when the season is done,
When the alternate prayers
For sun and for rain are counted,
When the pain of weeding
And the pride of watching are through,
I will hold you high,
A shining sheaf
Above the thousand seeds grown wild.
Not by our planting,
But by heaven,
Our harvest.
Our own child.[19]

PART FIVE

MODERN LIFE

TECHNOLOGY: CONCEPTION AND TESTING

The Talmud says, "One who does not participate in 'be fruitful and multiply' causes God's presence to vanish." Judaism's fierce pronatalism has always been a source of pain to those who cannot fulfill the commandment to bear children, and infertility is an ancient and recurring theme. In the Bible, barrenness afflicts a striking number of the matriarchs, including Sarah, Rebecca, Rachel and Hannah. Rachel's anguished cry, "Give me children or I shall die," sounds all too familiar to infertile couples today.

While divine intervention was the cure for biblical infertility, today we seek solutions in doctors' offices and hospitals. And there, Jewish law enthusiastically applies the biblical imperative to heal the sick to fertility problems.

There is nearly universal Jewish support for virtually all technologies where the parents are the sources of egg and sperm: from testing and drug treatments, to surgery that clears blocked fallopian tubes, to *in vitro* fertilization. The single Jewish caveat is a concern for the privacy of individuals and couples. Judaism has always viewed the act of making love as sacred and private. Additionally, the tradition stresses modesty, decorum and respect. Couples undergoing the potentially embarrassing and emotionally taxing procedures of infertility testing and treatment are well advised to recall Judaism's demand for a special measure of compassion and consideration for this invasion, albeit consented to, of their privacy.

However, when infertility technology moves beyond the closed system of a married couple, Jewish law is not nearly so clear about what is permissible and what is not. Present-day Jewish physicians, rabbis, and ethicists are confronting developments such as sperm and egg harvesting and transplantation, and producing a wide range of opinion regarding the appropriateness of methods that involve the genetic materials and bodies of people outside a married couple.

A broad range of responses can be found in all segments of the Jewish world. There are Jewish supporters from all denominations of artificial insemination with donor sperm, and surrogate mothers as legitimate "last resorts" for infertile couples. There are equally diverse voices decrying these practices as destructive of families, as adulterous, and as fundamentally unethical. It is beyond the scope of this book to resolve these issues, or even to treat them in detail. There are, however, ethical dimensions to these new technologies that deserve careful consideration. Thoughtful consultation with a compatible rabbi, as well as physicians, may help in your deliberations.

TAY-SACHS

Tay-Sachs disease is an inherited disorder of the nervous system that is one hundred times more common in Ashkenazic Jewish children than in non-Jewish children. By the age of about six months, a baby with Tay-Sachs disease loses physical skills, sight, and the ability to eat or smile. There is no known cure for the disease, and death usually occurs by four years of age.

The cause of Tay-Sachs disease is the absence of a vital enzyme (Hex A), which the body uses to break down fatty substances (lipids) in the brain. Without the Hex A enzyme, lipids accumulate and eventually destroy brain function.

Carriers of Tay-Sachs are detected by means of a blood test. When both parents carry the gene for Tay-Sachs, there is a one in four chance that a pregnancy will result in an afflicted baby. Some couples, upon learning that any pregnancy has a 25 percent chance of resulting in a Tay-Sachs baby, choose to adopt. For those who wish to conceive, prenatal testing is a second line of prevention.

Amniocentesis (removal of a small quantity of fluid from the uterus early in the second trimester of pregnancy) can determine whether or not the fetus has Tay-Sachs. The pregnancy may then be terminated.

Jewish law has long sanctioned the practice of abortion, in some cases. Even the most conservative interpretation of *halachah* allows abortion to save the life of the mother. More liberal positions permit abortion if the birth would cause the mother mental anguish and suffering. In cases where there is evidence of prenatal defects or genetic disease, Jewish law sanctions abortion not from the perspective of the child, but in order to spare the mother pain at raising such a child.

For more information about not only Tay-Sachs, but also a group of rarer genetic conditions that affect Jews, contact: The National Tay-Sachs and Allied Diseases Association, 385 Elliot Street, Newton MA 02164. 617-964-5508.

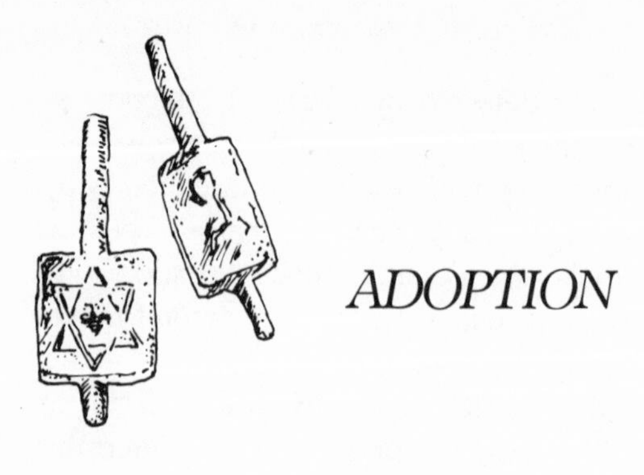

ADOPTION

If you turned to this chapter first, you probably already know the statistics; as many as one in six American couples may have difficulty conceiving. The medical and sociological causes of infertility are being studied and debated in many quarters. But for a variety of reasons, more and more American Jews are turning to adoption as a way of including children in their families, and of fulfilling the *mitzvah* of *pe'ru ur-vu,* be fruitful and multiply.

If you *are* starting with this chapter, remember that the rest of this book is also for you. While this section focuses on issues specific to adoption, the sections on names, *brit* or covenant ceremonies, celebrations, and announcements apply to all new parents, whether you meet your bundle of joy in a delivery room, at an airport or in an office.

For many people, adoption is a difficult choice, a last resort. The decision may even represent a kind of loss, compared by some to the pain felt at the death of a loved one; it means acknowledging that you do not expect to ever have a child of your own flesh. Thoughtful adoption professionals feel that many people need to grieve that loss before looking ahead to adoption.

The process of adopting is anything but simple. It begins with questions and paperwork; and then there is the long wait. International or domestic? Through an agency or privately? Infant or older child? Fortunately, you do not have to make these decisions alone. There is a large and growing network of people who have been there before you and can guide and comfort you through the process.

Adoption is no longer a rarity in the Jewish world, nor is it a shame or stigma best kept secret from the child and the community. The emerging Jewish view of adoption is best put by Rabbi Daniel Shevitz, the father of two adopted sons, whose writings and comments inform much of this chapter: "As long as there are children in need of homes, and loving homes in need of children, adoption should be encouraged as an act of piety and love."[1]

And as any adoptive parent can tell you, there is no difference between *naches* (the special joy children give their parents) from adopted children and *naches* from biological children.

JUDAISM AND ADOPTION

The most famous "adoptee" in Jewish tradition is Moses, who was raised by Pharaoh's daughter and turned out very well indeed. But neither biblical nor rabbinic Judaism provide much guidance for modern couples considering adoption.

The Jewish law on adoption is sketchy, lacking any mention of specific rules or legal procedures. Still, *halachah* provided for the care of needy children, pronouncing, "The court is father to all orphans and must pursue their benefit."[2] Indeed, the rabbis looked kindly on the actions of Pharaoh's daughter and it has always been considered a *mitzvah*—a good and holy act—to take orphaned children into one's home. And despite the law's recognition of certain immutable ties to birth parents, foster or adoptive parents assumed all the burdens and the rewards of parenthood. Hence the saying, those who raise a child are called its parents, and not the ones who conceived it.

What little *halachah* there is on the subject of adoption relates to Jewish orphans, who were most likely to require assistance from the Jewish community.[3] Today, however, the release of

Jewish children is extremely rare, so American Jews are far more concerned with practices relating to the adoption of non-Jewish children.

ADOPTION AND CONVERSION

According to Jewish law, a baby born of a non-Jewish mother is not considered Jewish and must be converted by *mikvah* (ritual immersion) for both girls and boys, and *brit milah* for boys.* Both acts require the presence of a *bet din,* a rabbinical court of three.

An uncircumcised adopted male newborn may be given a *brit milah* on the eighth day after birth, or as soon as possible thereafter, in the presence of a *bet din,* one of whom is generally the *mohel.* For the baby adopted at four months or older, it is common to have the procedure done in a hospital, with anesthetic and the supervision of a physician. In such cases, both a pediatrician and a *mohel* are consulted.

If the child was circumcised as an infant without religious ceremony, a ritual called *hatafat dam brit,* is performed. Here, the *mohel* draws a drop of blood from the site of the circumcision. This ceremony is easily done in the home or synagogue, regardless of the child's age. The chapter on *brit milah* contains a full discussion of the practice, laws, and customs pertaining to circumcision, including a special section on *bris* for conversion and adoption.

Mikvah is required of all converts to Judaism, male and female, adults and children of all ages. Immersion in a *mikvah* is a form of renewal and rebirth. The water of the ritual bath recalls the mystical source of all water and thus all life—the river whose

* *The Reform and Reconstructionist movements, however, recognize as Jews children with one Jewish parent—*father *or* mother*—who are then given a Jewish home and education. The differences between liberal and traditional Jewish practice regarding conversion is discussed later in this chapter.*

source is Eden.[4] The *mayim hayyim,* or living water, of *mikvah* also represents the physical source of human life, the waters of the womb.

Immersion must be total, as it was in the womb. Nothing may be interposed between the body and the water, so the naked child is held loosely and lowered into the water. One of the child's new parents, or a relative or friend, thus "births" the baby as a Jew.

If you live in a temperate climate or if the adoption of your child occurs during the summer, it is perfectly kosher to do *mikvah* in any body of *mayim hayyim,* living or running water. Ponds, lakes, rivers, and seas are natural *mikvaot.* For many, natural bodies of water provide a more spiritually satisfying experience than an indoor bath; however, weather, family custom or rabbinical preference may discourage this option.

Your rabbi will convene a *bet din,* a court of three observant individuals or rabbis, to witness the immersion. When the child is raised from the water, the following blessing is recited by one of the rabbis or by a family member:

בָּרוּךְ אַתָּה יְיָ, אֱלֹהֵינוּ מֶלֶךְ הָעוֹלָם אֲשֶׁר קִדְּשָׁנוּ בְּמִצְוֹתָיו, וְצִוָּנוּ עַל הַטְּבִילָה.

Baruch ata Adonai Eloheynu Melech Ha-olam asher kid'shanu, be-mitzvotav vitsivanu al ha'tevilah.

Praised are you, Adonai, God of all creation who sanctifies us with your commandments and commands us concerning immersion.

The *shehehiyanu* is then recited.

For boys, a *mikvah* appointment is scheduled sometime after the circumcision has healed. Remember, though, that *brit milah* or *mikvah* are delayed if there is any suspicion of a health risk.

For girls, *mikvah* is the only ritual requirement. Baby girls are named following *mikvah,* either immediately after immersion or sometime later in a ceremony at a synagogue or at home. The chapter on *brit habat* contains many suggestions for celebrating the arrival of a daughter into your lives and into the covenant of the Jewish people.

While circumcision is performed at the earliest possible date, there is some difference of opinion regarding *mikvah.* It is not uncommon to take newborns to the *mikvah.* One father counsels blowing into the baby's face as she is dunked, which he claims makes the child hold her breath for the few seconds of immersion. However, according to other sources, immersion is not done until the baby is three years old,[5] and some rabbis even recommend reserving *mikvah* for much later. Indeed, some parents and rabbis suggest that *mikvah* take place when the child is preparing for his or her *bar* or *bat mitzvah,* so it becomes an intentional rite of passage for a young person preparing to receive and accept the responsibilities of the Torah.

This approach dovetails with Talmudic law regarding converted children, for whom the process is not completed until maturity (traditionally, thirteen years old for boys, twelve for girls). At this time, the child has the right to renounce—or affirm—his or her Jewish identity. Legally, the right to renounce expires when a child reaches adulthood; however, since renunciation is based on the child's knowledge of her origins, if the adoption has been kept a secret, she cannot decide, and thus her Jewish status is not settled.

There are serious objections to this practice, on both *halachic* and psychological grounds. Without *mikvah* an adopted child is not legally Jewish. And a formal reminder at the age of twelve or thirteen, that he is not *really* Jewish can cause distress. This is often a time when identity issues are coming to the fore; adoption creates enough cause for ambiguity that conversion should not be added to it. A simple declaration of one's Jewish identity at *bar* or *bat mitzvah* is sufficient acknowledgment of the Talmudic right to renounce.

Whatever you decide to do about *mikvah,* there is widespread support among adoption professionals, Jewish and non-Jewish, for full disclosure about your child's origins from the beginning. In the case of international or interracial adoption, there is often no question of concealment, but the same principles apply even if the child resembles his adoptive parents. The story of how Mommy and Daddy waited and hoped for little Sarah's arrival, complete pictures of their meeting—these become part of the child's sense of who she is and how she belongs.

WHO IS A JEW?

Although the tradition views *mikvah* and *milah* as essential, some liberal rabbis dispense with ritual circumcision in the case of already circumcised boys, and others disapprove of immersion for infants and children altogether. These positions are extremely controversial in the American Jewish community, and also in Israel. The debate is an old one: the authority of *halachah* in the modern world.

But even if your Reform, Conservative, or Reconstructionist rabbi follows the law to the letter, convening a *bet din* for a child's *milah* and/or *mikvah* as required, there are rabbis who may not recognize your son or daughter as a kosher Jew. (This is true for adult conversions as well.) Unless the rituals are supervised and witnessed by Orthodox rabbis, your child's conversion may be challenged as inauthentic by the Orthodox community. Given the current religious-political debate in the state of Israel, a non-Orthodox conversion may, at some point, impugn your child's status as a Jew and a citizen there. For this reason, some liberal Jews seek out Orthodox rabbis to oversee the conversion of their children, just to make sure that nobody, in any Jewish community anywhere, can question their identity.

The overwhelming majority of Jews have their sons circumcised as infants, a practice that is followed with adopted infant sons. However, if the child is much older, circumcision is a far more difficult decision to make—and explain. The fear and pain associated with having the procedure done on a school-age boy cannot be wished away, and some parents refuse to subject their new son to such a bewildering operation. But for others, a decision not to circumcise seems just as wrong. One adoptive parent wrote eloquently of her decision to have two sons, ages seven and eleven, circumcised: "We considered letting the boys grow up and make the decision for themselves. It would have been an easier way out for us as parents. . . . I felt it would have made being Jewish a possibility for the future for them, not a reality in the present . . . I truly feared that it might make them hate Judaism, not to mention make them hate us. I could only say to them that if I did not have them circumcised, I would not be treating them like my true sons . . . the same as if they had been born to me as babies."[6]

PROBLEMS AND SERVICES

In certain periods of Jewish history, the biological or racial aspect of Jewish peoplehood was considered paramount. The same racial definition of Judaism that has been the pretext for so much anti-Semitism is still alive within the Jewish community. While overt racism is, by and large, socially unacceptable, there are many among us who fear and reject people—even children—who look "different." This fear finds expression in everything from the garden-variety cruelty that kids display on the playground, to the grandma who worries (aloud) that her granddaughter might one day grow up to marry the Korean-born Rosenbloom kid.

But the Jewish people, *am yisrael,* is a changing people, and as it changes, the old prejudices will wither. Just as modern Israel includes black-skinned Ethiopian Jews and blue-eyed refuseniks, the American Jewish community of the twenty-first century will include taller and blonder, dark-skinned and almond-eyed Jews. Besides, we are, as we always have been, not a race but a people who choose to enter into a special relationship with God. As Rabbi Daniel Shevitz has written, the most important aspect of Jewish self-definition has always been the covenant, "the bonds of promise, service and expectation between God and Israel, that make one a true member of the Jewish community."[7]

While all Jewish parents worry about their children's commitment to Judaism as adults (will they identify as Jews? will they intermarry?), adoptive parents may be particularly sensitive to the difficulties their kids may face as adolescents and later in life. Indeed, some parents feel guilty about asking a child to assume the burden of belonging to two minority groups. One adoptive parent writes, "I'm sure that little voices inside each of them were saying something to the effect, 'Millions of American families and we had to get Jews.' "

The first line of support for any major life change is your community, family and friends, synagogue or *havurah*. And today, agencies that deal with adoption now tend to offer support services that extend long past the day the baby is legally yours. (When you are choosing an adoption agency or service, you should feel comfortable asking any and all questions—including concerns about raising a Guatemalan-born Jew in Springfield, Illinois.)

Professional services to meet the specific needs of Jewish adoptive families are just beginning to come of age. Jewish family agencies vary greatly in terms of sensitivity and expertise; some barely acknowledge the special concerns and growing numbers of adopting couples, while others provide a wide range of support services for adoptive families, from help with special-needs children, to family counseling, to Chanukah parties.

All members of adoptive families benefit from contact with other parents and children who share similar histories, questions and challenges. Just being part of a group of families who look like yours is an important form of validation. And today there is Stars of David.

Stars of David is a national nonprofit social support network for Jewish adoptive families. Founded in 1984, Stars of David grew from one adoptive family to five hundred families nationwide in less than three years. Chapters have been formed in cities from Connecticut to Oregon, and members include Jews of all affiliations, intermarried couples, single parents, prospective parents, interracial couples with biological children, and grandparents. While Stars of David is *not* an adoption agency, everyone who joins agrees to have his or her name published on the national list and thus become a resource for other members.

For more information about Stars of David, contact Phyllis Nissen or Rabbi Susan Abramson at Temple Shalom Emeth, 16 Lexington Street, Burlington MA 01803, (617) 272-2351. (Please remember, Stars of David is *not* an adoption agency.)

And as adoption becomes an ever more common phenomenon in the Jewish community, there will be other resources, like *Chag Sameach!,* a children's book that celebrates the racial and ethnic variety of American Jews. On the cover a Caucasian man wearing *kippah* and *tallit* blows a *shofar,* while a little Asian girl, also holding a *shofar,* looks up at him lovingly.[8]

NAMES

There is usually no difference in the way adoptive parents and birth parents select names. When American Jews adopt, their children are commonly named in memory of family members who have died. Typically, a child's full Hebrew name includes his or her parents' names as well, as in *David ben Moshe v'Rivka,* David the son of Moses and Ruth; or *Gila bat Raphael v'Leah,* or Gila, the daughter of Raphael and Leah. Sometimes, however, the custom for adult converts is followed: *David ben Avraham Aveinu v'Sara Amenu,* David the son of Abraham our father and Sarah our mother. This "generic" convert's name was more common in the past, when the adopted child was likely to be a born Jew. Since ritual status—like that of *kohane* and *levi*—is inherited biologically, the rabbis wanted to be certain there would be no confusion if a child took the last name of his Cohen or Levinson adoptive parents.

CEREMONIES

The adoption of a child is a rite of passage as momentous as a birth and deserves the same kind of attention and care we lavish on all joyous life cycle events. Any and all ceremonies related to adoption—*brit milah, mikvah,* naming—may be the occasion for a meaningful, personal celebration. Or you might want to consider a Jewish ceremony that sanctifies the act of adoption itself.

Since some communities harbor vestiges of the old belief that adoption is somehow an embarrassment that should be concealed, your celebration can help lay old prejudices to rest, showing your family, friends, and community how you feel about the blessing, joy, and opportunity of holiness that attend the adoption of a child. A written guide to your ceremony will help guests follow along and participate in the proceedings.

The following ceremony is a model of a simple, moving Jewish adoption ceremony. The chapters on *brit milah, brit habat,* and *hiddur mitzvah* are also filled with ideas, prayers, and poems that are appropriate to celebrate and welcome the arrival of any child to the Jewish people.

BRIT IMMUTS
Covenant of Adoption[9]
for Noah Hernan

Noah is escorted into the room by his paternal grandmother and given to his maternal grandmother. The parents explain the nature of the ceremony and tell the story of the baby's name. Verses from Psalm 119 spelling out Noah in Hebrew are recited in Hebrew and English by family and friends.

Noah is placed on the knees of his adoptive parents, who then take the following oath.

נִשְׁבָּעִים אֲנַחְנוּ בְּשֵׁם מִי שֶׁשְּׁמוֹ רַחוּם וְחַנּוּן שֶׁנְּקַיֵּים אֶת הַיֶּלֶד/הַיַּלְדָּה הַזֶּה/הַזֹּאת כְּאִילוּ הָיָה/הָיְתָה מִזַּרְעֵנוּ יוֹצֵא/יוֹצְאת חֲלָצֵנוּ. וּנְגַדְּלוֹ/וּנְגַדְּלָהּ/וְנַחֲזִיקָהּ וְנַדְרִיכוֹ/וְנַדְרִיכָהּ בְּדַרְכֵי תּוֹרָתֵנוּ, כְּכָל מִצְוֹת הַבֵּן/הַבַּת עַל הָאָב וְהָאֵם. יְהִי ה׳ אֱלֹהֵינוּ עִמּוֹ/עִמָּהּ בְּכָל מַעֲשֵׂה יָדָיו/יָדֶיהָ. אָמֵן, כֵּן יְהִי רָצוֹן.

We solemnly swear, by the One who is called loving and merciful, that we will raise this child as our own. We will nurture him, sustain him, and guide him in the paths of Torah, in accordance with the duties incumbent upon Jewish parents. May God ever be with him. We pray for the wisdom and strength to help our child, Noah Hernan, and his brother, Joshua Simon Luis, become men of integrity and kindness.

הַמַּלְאָךְ הַגֹּאֵל אֹתִי מִכָּל־רָע יְבָרֵךְ אֶת־הַנְּעָרִים וְיִקָּרֵא בָהֶם שְׁמִי וְשֵׁם אֲבֹתַי אַבְרָהָם וְיִצְחָק וְיִדְגּוּ לָרֹב בְּקֶרֶב הָאָרֶץ׃

May the One who saved me from all evil, bless these lads, and let them be called by our name and the names of our ancestors and may they multiply throughout the land.*

For a girl, you might substitute the following:

בְּרוּכָה אַתְּ לַיהוָה בִּתִּי וְעַתָּה בִּתִּי אַל תִּירְאִי כֹּל אֲשֶׁר תֹּאמְרִי אֶעֱשֶׂה לָּךְ כִּי אֵשֶׁת חַיִל תִּהְיִי.

Be blessed of the Lord, daughter! And now, daughter, have no fear. I will do in your behalf whatever you ask, for you will be a fine woman. (Ruth 3:10–11)

* *The prayer recited by the patriarch Jacob when he adopted his two grandsons, Menashe and Ephraim.*

The blessing of peace is given, followed by the *shehehiyanu,* recited by all.

Noah's grandfather and a friend give the child blessings from family and community.

The company joins in the singing of *Yona matz'a,* which refers to Noah's dove, who found peace on the Sabbath.

Kiddush is recited, and brunch served. Words of Torah from an honored friend are offered before the singing of *birkat hamazon,* the blessing after meals.

ANNOUNCEMENTS

The joy of welcoming an adopted child into your family deserves to be shared with relatives and friends. An adoption announcement can also answer many questions about your new baby. For suggestions about thoughtful ways to spread your wonderful news, as well as general information about producing a distinctively Jewish announcement, see the section on Announcements.

PART SIX

THE FIRST YEAR

THE FIRST YEAR

The first year of a child's life is a series of milestones for the entire family. The first smile, the first step, the first word, all are dutifully recorded in a journal and breathlessly reported to doting grandparents and half-interested friends alike.

The first year of a Jewish baby's life is also a series of *shehehiyanus*—the prayer of thanksgiving that greets all sorts of milestones—from the first full night's sleep to your child's first Passover seder. As the seasons change during your child's first year, the holidays are experienced and remembered differently; giving Jonathan his first applesauce on Rosh Hashana; trying to get Dan to look at the blazing lights on the eighth night of Çhanukah; hauling Shira's diaper bag and playpen to a Purim party.

Most of all, though, Shabbat changes. Not only is your experience of rest and relaxation altered forever, the observance of the Sabbath changes as well. Many families have discovered the old custom of adding a candle for each child. And the traditional blessing over your children reminds everyone, no matter how tired or aggravated you are with each other, of the love that makes you a family.

Laying a hand on a child's head, the father and/or mother says:

For girls: יְשִׂמֵךְ אֱלֹהִים כְּשָׂרָה, רִבְקָה, רָחֵל וְלֵאָה.

Y'seemech Eloheem k'Sara, Rivka, Rachel v'Leah.

May God make you as Sarah, Rebecca, Rachel and Leah.*

For boys:

יְשִׂמְךָ אֱלֹהִים כְּאֶפְרַיִם וְכִמְנַשֶּׁה.

Y'seem-cha Eloheem k'Efrayim v'chee Menashe.

May God make you as Ephraim and Menasheh.†

Followed by the priestly blessing:

יְבָרֶכְךָ יְיָ וְיִשְׁמְרֶךָ. יָאֵר יְיָ פָּנָיו אֵלֶיךָ וִיחֻנֶּךָּ. יִשָּׂא יְיָ פָּנָיו אֵלֶיךָ וְיָשֵׂם לְךָ שָׁלוֹם.

May Adonai bless you and protect you. May Adonai shine the countenance upon you and be gracious to you. May Adonai favor you and grant you peace.

This custom suggests others; in one family, parents take the opportunity to say how something their children learned or did or said in the past week made them proud.

Some parents celebrate their child's first birthday by planting a tree, or with a gift of *tsedakah.* If you created a *wimpel,* Torah binder, to honor your child's *brit,* it is customary to bring the completed band to your synagogue on or near the child's first birthday as a gift to the congregation. (The *wimpel* will be used on the Torah on the occasion of your baby's *bar* or *bat mitzvah.*[1])

WEANING

Nursing is a powerful connection between mother and child, and its end is a milestone for both. In the past few years, weaning

* *The matriarchs of Judaism.*
† *The sons of Joseph and Osenath.*

has become the occasion for Jewish celebrations that hark back to Judaism's first baby and also embody contemporary Jewish women's spirituality. Indeed, there is no mention of a *simcha* in honor of Isaac's circumcision; the Torah says, "And the child grew and was weaned and Abraham made a feast on the day Isaac was weaned."

Weaning may have been celebrated with more ceremony than birth or circumcision for generations. A child who survived infancy to the time of weaning—sometimes two or three years—had demonstrated viability and vitality. In the Bible, Hannah's prayer of thanksgiving was offered after Samuel's weaning, not after his birth.

Even rabbinic literature notes the importance of the nursing relationship, using it as a metaphor for the bond between God and the people of Israel. Indeed, the *midrash* compares the giving of the Torah at Sinai to a nursing mother.[2]

Contemporary weaning celebrations tend to be brief and simple, consisting of a series of prayers, personal reflections and commentary, and a meal. Since weaning and the introduction of solid foods may take months, a celebration like this will occur sometime during that process—whenever you feel it is time to observe this very personal rite of passage.

Commonly, weaning celebrations occur at home on Shabbat, either as part of lunch or incorporated into the ceremony that ends the day—*havdalah. Havdalah,* which means separation, is a recurrent theme of weaning celebrations. As the weekly *havdalah* sanctifies and celebrates the difference between sacred and secular time, weaning marks the second physical separation of mother and child.

It is customary to begin the meal at a weaning celebration by having someone other than the mother feed the child his or her first solid food. (A symbolic "first" is fine too. If your baby has already tasted rice cereal, offer a first taste of barley cereal or challah.) The honor of feeding the baby might be given to the father, a sibling or a grandparent. Another custom associated with this rediscovered rite of passage is the giving of *tsedakah* in the amount of the baby's weight, often to a charity having to do with hunger or children.

Weaning celebrations can be as simple as the addition of a *shehehiyanu* at the first Shabbat night meal after which the baby has not nursed for a full week. Or you can make weaning a more public milestone, complete with invitations and a printed program of readings, songs, and blessings.

The ceremony might reprise lines or readings from your child's *brit* ceremony, reflecting on the distance between that day and this. And the familiar lines from Ecclesiastes seem particularly appropriate at weaning.

A season is set for everything, a time for every experience under heaven:
A time for being born and a time for dying,
A time for planting and a time for uprooting the planted;
A time for slaying and a time for healing,
A time for tearing down and a time for building up;
A time for weeping and a time for laughing,
A time for wailing and a time for dancing;
A time for throwing stones and a time for gathering stones,
A time for embracing and a time for shunning embraces;
A time for seeking and a time for losing,
A time for keeping and a time for discarding;
A time for ripping and a time for sewing,
A time for silence and a time for speaking;
A time for loving and a time for hating;
A time for war and a time for peace.

Virtually all weaning celebrations include *kiddush* and the *shehehiyanu.* Some parents use white wine for the blessing, symbolizing mother's milk. And if the baby has not already been given a *kiddush* cup, this might be a nice occasion to buy one for your son or daughter, and to offer him or her a sip from it. And the ceremony that follows has a big, fun finish.

YONA'S BIRTHDAY PARTY-WEANING[3]

Parents:

Just as Abraham and Sarah rejoiced at the weaning of their son Isaac, our hearts too are glad that Yona has grown into full childhood, sustained in good health by God's gift of milk.

Mother:

בָּרוּךְ אַתָּה יְיָ אֱלֹהֵינוּ מֶלֶךְ הָעוֹלָם אֲשֶׁר פָּתַח אֶת שָׁדַי וְהֵנַקְתִּי אֶת פְּרִי רַחְמִי

Blessed are you, God, ruler of the universe, who opened my breasts to nurse the fruit of my womb.

Father:

בָּרוּךְ אַתָּה יְיָ אֱלֹהֵינוּ מֶלֶךְ הָעוֹלָם מְשַׂמֵּחַ הוֹרִים בְּיַלְדֵיהֶם.

Blessed are you, God, ruler of the universe, who enables parents to rejoice in their children.

Together:

In love, we will continue to give sustenance to our child and provide for her physical needs. May we also provide her with spiritual sustenance through examples of lovingkindness and through the teaching of Torah and the traditions of our people.

A donation of $25, equal to Yona's weight, has been made to *Maon Latinok,* a home for the care of infants with Down's Syndrome, in Israel.

Today, we present Yona with a *kiddush* cup, symbolizing her independence from the breast and the hope that she will grow to participate in the *mitzvah* of *kiddush.*

Kiddush is recited.

Hand washing.

Motzi.

Father feeds Yona a piece of challah, symbolizing her independence from mother's milk, and his now-equal responsibility for nourishing her.

Parents break a baby bottle.

The company shouts: *Mazel Tov!*

DIRECTORY OF CALLIGRAPHERS

There are calligraphers working in both Hebrew and English in most American cities. This list is not comprehensive; it simply includes artists known to me, whose work includes birth announcements on commission. All the calligraphers whose creations appear in this book are listed here.

Elaine Adler
3 Sunny Knoll Terrace
Lexington MA 02173

Rose Ann Chasman
6300 Whipple
Chicago IL 60659

Peggy H. Davis
3249 Hennepin Ave So. Suite 144
Minneapolis MN 55408

Shendl Diamond
12203 Leona Lane
Poway CA 92064

Sara Glaser
31 Glenwood Avenue
Oakland CA 94611

Jay Greenspan
PO Box 914
Cathedral Station
New York NY 10025

Shonna Husbands-Hankin
1176 Lorane Highway
Eugene OR 97405

Jonathan Kremer
35 East Athens Avenue
Ardmore PA 19003

Susan Leviton
3417 North 4th Street
Harrisburg PA 17110

Grace Perlman Miller
7205 Lincoln Drive
Philadelphia PA 19119

Sara Novenson
200 East 16th Street, Apt 16A
New York NY 10003

Jeanette Kuvin Oren
13 Great Pines Court
Rockville MD 20850

Naomi Teplow
1518 Excelsior Avenue
Oakland CA 94602

Betsy Platkin Teutsch
629 West Cliveden Street
Philadelphia PA 19119-3651

GLOSSARY

ALEPH-BET Name of the Hebrew alphabet; also, its first two letters.
ALIYAH Literally, "to go up": to be called to the Torah. Also, *making aliyah* refers to moving to the land of Israel.
APOCRYPHA Fourteen "writings," including the Book of Tobit, that were not included in the final redaction of the Bible, but which are, nevertheless, important Jewish texts.
ARAMAIC Semitic language closely related to Hebrew, the lingua franca of the Middle East. The Talmud was written in Aramaic.
ASHKENAZIC Jews and Jewish culture of Eastern and Central Europe.
AUFRUF Recognition given when a groom or a couple is called up to the Torah on the Shabbat before a wedding.
BAAL SHEM TOV Israel ben Eliezer, the founder of Hasidism, the eighteenth-century mystical revival movement.
BARUCH ATA ADONAI Words that begin Hebrew blessings, most commonly rendered in English as "Blessed art Thou, Lord our God, King of the Universe." This book contains many alternatives to that translation.
BAT Daughter, or daughter of, as in *bat mitzvah,* daughter of the commandment.
B.C.E. Before the Common Era. Jews avoid the Christian designation B.C., which means Before Christ.

BIMAH Raised platform in the synagogue from which the Torah and prayers are read.
BRIS/BRIT MILAH The covenant of circumcision. *Bris* is the Ashkenazic spelling.
BRIT Covenant, and covenant ceremony.
C.E. Common era.
CHALLAH Braided loaf of egg bread, traditional for Shabbat, the holidays, and festive occasions.
CONSERVATIVE Religious movement, developed in the United States during the 19th century as a more traditional response to modernity than offered by Reform.
DAVEN Pray.
DIASPORA Exile. The dwelling of Jews outside the Holy Land.
D'RASH Religious insight, often on a text from the Torah.
DREYDL A top used for playing a game of chance during the festival of Chanukah.
D'VAR TORAH Literally, "words of Torah": an explication of a portion of the Torah. (Plural: divrei)
EREV Hebrew, "evening." Erev Shabbat is Friday night.
FLAYSHIG Meat food, which, according to *kashrut,* may not be mixed with dairy products.
HAGGADAH The book containing the liturgy of the Passover seder.
HAIMISH Yiddish for homelike, giving one a sense of belonging.
HALACHAH Jewish law.
HASIDISM Eighteenth-century mystical revival movement that stressed God's immanence in the world. The doctrine of *simcha,* or joy, was taught as a way of communing with God.
HAVDALAH Hebrew for separation. Saturday evening ceremony that separates Shabbat from the rest of the week.
HAVURAH Literally, "fellowship." Also, small, participatory groups that meet for prayer, study, and celebration.
HAZZAN Cantor.
HUPPAH Wedding canopy.
KASHRUT System of laws that govern what and how Jews eat.
KETUBAH Marriage contract.
KIDDUSH Sanctification, and specifically the blessing over wine recited on Friday night, Shabbat, and other occasions.
KOHANE/KOHEN A member of the priestly tribe.
KOSHER Foods deemed fit for consumption according to the laws of *kashrut.*
KVATTER, KVATTERIN Godfather, godmother.
MAVEN An expert.
MAZEL TOV Literally, "good luck." In practice it means "congratulations."
MENSCH Person; an honorable, decent person.
MESADER One who "orders" or leads a ceremony.
MEZUZAH First two paragraphs of the *Shema* written on a parchment

scroll and encased in a small container (*bayit*), affixed to the doorposts of a home.

MIDRASH A body of literature consisting of imaginative exposition of and stories based on holy scriptures.

MIKVAH Ritual bath.

MILAH Circumcision, *brit milah* is the covenant of circumcision.

MILCHIG Dairy foods, which, according to *kashrut,* may not be mixed with meat products.

MINHAG Custom (plural: *minhagim*).

MINYAN A prayer quorum of ten adult Jews—for traditional Jews, ten men.

MISHNA The first part of the Talmud, comprised of six "orders" of laws regarding everything from agriculture to marriage.

MOHEL One who is trained in the rituals and procedures of *brit milah,* circumcision.

MOTZI Blessing over bread recited before meals.

NACHES Special joy from the achievements of one's children.

NIGGUN A wordless prayerlike melody.

ORTHODOX Generally, strictly observant, traditional. The modern Orthodox movement developed in the nineteenth century.

PARASHA Weekly Torah portion.

PESACH Passover.

PIDYON HABEN The ceremony of redeeming the firstborn son.

RABBI Teacher. Today, rabbi refers to a seminary ordained member of the clergy. "The rabbis" refers to the men who codified the Talmud.

RECONSTRUCTIONIST Religious movement, begun in the United States in the twentieth century by Mordecai M. Kaplan, that views Judaism as an evolving religious civilization.

REFORM A movement, begun in nineteenth-century Germany, that sought to reconcile Jewish tradition with modernity. Reform Judaism disputes the divine authority of *halachah.*

ROSH HODESH First day of every lunar month; the New Month, a semiholiday.

SANDEK Godfather; the one who holds the baby during the circumcision. *Sandeket* is a new term for godmother.

S'EUDAT MITZVAH A commanded meal; the festive celebration of a milestone.

SHABBAT Sabbath. In Yiddish, Shabbos.

SHECHINA The divine presence, generally described with feminine imagery.

SHEHEHIYANU A prayer of thanksgiving.

SHEMA The most often recited Jewish prayer that declares God's Oneness.

SHEVA B'RACHOT Seven marriage blessings.

SHTETL Small town, especially one inhabited by Ashkenazic Jews before the Holocaust.

SHUL Synagogue.

SIDDUR Daily and Shabbat prayer book.
SIMCHA Joy and the celebration of joy. (Plural is *simchot.*)
TAHARAT HAMISHPAHAH Laws of family purity prescribing sexual availability and the use of *mikvah.*
TALLIS/TALLIT Prayer shawl.
TALMUD Collection of rabbinic thought and laws from 200 B.C.E. to 500 C.E.
TIKKUN OLAM Repairing the world. A fundamental Jewish concept of taking responsibility for the temporal world.
TORAH First five books of the Hebrew Bible, portions of which are read every Shabbat.
TSEDAKAH Righteous giving, charity.
YICHUS Family status. Pride in family member's achievements.
YIDDISH Language spoken by Ashkenazic Jews, a combination of early German and Hebrew.
YOM KIPPUR Day of Atonement, the holiest of the High Holy Days.

NOTES

PART ONE: CHAI: LIFE

Conception

1. For a fuller explanation of *mikvah,* see Anita Diamant, *The New Jewish Wedding.* New York: Summit Books, 1985, p. 150.
2. Mark Zborowski and Elizabeth Herzog, *Life Is with People.* New York: Schocken Books, 1952, p. 312.
3. Barbara Rosman Penzner and Amy Zweiback-Levenson, "Spiritual Cleansing: A Mikvah Ritual for Brides." *Reconstructionist Magazine,* September 1986, pp. 25–28.

Pregnancy

4. Zborowski and Herzog, pp. 313–317. Lilith, Adam's first wife, was punished for her behavior to the first man with the awful fate of having to give birth to multitudes of demon babies who were then murdered daily. She took her revenge, so went the superstition, by killing Jewish newborns.
5. Rabbi David Simcha Rosenthal, *A Joyful Mother of Children.* Jerusalem: Feldheim Publishers, Ltd., 1982.

6. ©Rabbi Judy Shanks, 1983. Recited as part of the *Sh'ma al Ha-Mitah*. Reprinted with permission of the author. Rabbi Maggie Wenig adapted this poem for use in a *brit habat* ceremony:

> With all my heart, with all my soul, with all my might I thank You, God, for the gift of this wonderful child. I thank You for a healthy pregnancy, a safe delivery and a speedy recovery.
>
> With all my heart, with all my soul, with all my might
> I pray for the continued health of this child.
> I pray for her to be strong in mind and body,
> To grow steadily and sturdily in a home filled with joy.
> I pray for her to become a person who greets the world
> With passion, courage, humility, humor and patience.
>
> With all my heart, with all my soul, with all my might
> I pray for God to watch over me and my family.
> I pray for the ability to love and nurture this child
> To provide for her and to educate her,
> To understand her and to allow her the freedom to grow.

7. Penina V. Adelman, *Miriam's Well: Rituals for Jewish Women Around the Year*. Fresh Meadows, NY: Biblio Press, 1986.
8. These blessings were written by a group of women in New York who called themselves Bat Kol; they appeared in *Chutzpah*, July-August 1975, Chicago.
9. Zonderman, Shoshana. "SpiRitual preparation for parenthood." *Response*, Vol. XIV, No. 4. Spring, 1985, pp. 29–39.

Birth

10. According to tradition, the blessing said on the birth of a son is *Hatov ve-hamativ*; for a daughter, one says *shehehiyanu*. In practice, however, either or both blessings are recited. (See Rosenthal.)

PART TWO: NAMING YOUR JEWISH BABY

What's in a Name?

1. Nathan Gottlieb, *A Jewish Child Is Born*. New York: Bloch Publishing Co., 1960, p. 111.
2. Alfred Kolatch, *The Name Dictionary*. Middle Village, NY.: Jonathan David Publishers, 1967, p. xi.
3. Benzion C. Kaganoff, *A Dictionary of Jewish Names and Their History*. New York: Schocken Books, 1977, p. 49.
4. Kaganoff, p. 53.

5. Rabbi Herbert C. Dobrinski, *A Treasury of Sephardic Laws and Customs*. New York and Hoboken, NJ: Yeshiva University & Ktav, 1986, p. 4.
6. Dobrinski, p. 61.
7. Dobrinski, p. 4.
8. Matthew Nesvisky, "There's Miki, Riki, Tiki, Suki, Shuli, Tzippi, Tzuri, Uri and Nuri." *Moment Magazine*, Vol. 9, #8, September 1984/Elul 5744, pp. 47–51.

The Lists, and How to Use Them

9. Nesvisky, p. 50.

PART THREE: BRIT: COVENANT

Brit Milah: The Covenant of Circumcision

1. Exodus 4:24–25.
2. *Encyclopaedia Judaica*. Jerusalem: Ketter Publishing, 1972, p. 570.
3. Theodor H. Gaster, *The Holy and the Profane*. New York: W. Sloane Assoc., 1955, pp. 53–54.
4. Rabbi Paysach J. Krohn, *Bris Milah; Circumcision—The Covenant of Abraham*. Brooklyn NY: Mesorah Publications, 1969, pp. 62–63.
5. Krohn, pp. 131–132.
6. Betsy A. Lehman, "The Age-old Question of Circumcision," *The Boston Globe*, June 22, 1987.
7. Lehman. However, there is some evidence, published in the journal *Pediatrics* in 1985 and 1986, suggesting an increased risk of urinary tract infections in uncircumcised babies; studies showed that infection occurred in about 4 percent of boys who had not undergone the procedure, while circumcised boys had between 1/10th and 1/20th the rate of infection. Preliminary evidence suggests that circumcision may also provide some benefit in resisting infection with the AIDS virus.
8. Rabbi Lawrence Kushner, "Save This Article," Bulletin of Congregation Beth El of the Sudbury River Valley, Sudbury MA. Vol. VIII, No 6., Sivan/Tammuz 5742, p. 3.
9. Henry C. Romberg, MD. *Bris Milah*. New York and Jerusalem: Feldheim Publishers, Ltd., 1982, p. 94.

Studies of hospital circumcision have shown problems in less than 2 percent of all cases; serious complications are rarer still. *Mohels* claim that their circumcisions result in even fewer problems, a claim that cannot be substantiated, however.

10. Dr. Sheldon B. Korones, M.D., *High Risk Newborn Infants*, St. Louis MO: The C.V. Mosby Co., 1976.

11. The *halachically* prescribed practice of *metitzah*—the drawing of blood away from the wound—was, for centuries, accomplished with the lips. The erotic and homoerotic suggestions in that act are clearly disturbing. While many *mohels* now either omit *metitzah* or use a pipette to ritually remove the blood, *bris* remains a deeply unsettling event that few guests actually watch.
12. Midrash Tanchuma on *Tetzaveḥ*, 1.
13. Hayyim Schauss, *The Lifetime of a Jew Throughout the Ages of Jewish History*. New York: Union of American Hebrew Congregations, 1950, p. 33.
14. Schauss, p. 36–37.
15. Nathan Ausubel, *The Book of Jewish Knowledge*. New York: Crown Publishers, Inc., 1964, p. 114.
16. Krohn, p. 98.
17. Dobrinski, p. 7.
18. Schauss, p. 25.
19. Charles Weiss, "A Worldwide Survey of the Current Practice of Milah," *Jewish Social Studies*, Number 24, 1962, p. 43. The United Kingdom is one of very few places with a system for training and regulation of milah. Since 1745 in London *mohels* must pass both a medical examination and a test given by a religious court. New York City, however, does have a *milah* board.
20. Isserles, *Shulchan Aruch, Yore Deah* 264:1. "A man should seek around to find the best and most pious *mohel* and *sandek*."
21. Dobrinski, p. 6.
22. Krohn, p. 125.
23. Kushner, p. 3.
24. From a ceremony by Rabbi Edward Treister and Rochelle Treister, June 17, 1986, Houston, Texas.
25. This ceremony, written for the *bris* of Jacob Nathan Ritari, was the work of his parents, Stephanie and Philip Ritari. Aliza Arzt worked on the traditional text, including equalizing the gender in Hebrew and English, and adding biblical verses, such as those mentioning "circumcision of the heart."
26. By Rabbi Sandy Eisenberg Sasso, from an unpublished manuscript in preparation for requirements toward a Doctor of Ministry project for Christian Theological Seminary in Indianapolis, and as part of her proposed birth section for the Reconstructionist Rabbi's Manual. An earlier version was published in a pamphlet entitled *Call Them Builders: A Resource Booklet About Jewish Attitudes and Practices on Birth and Family Life*. New York: Reconstructionist Federation of Congregations and Havurot, 1977.

Brit Habat: Welcoming Our Daughters

I have tried to give credit to everyone whose words appear in this chapter. However, because of the amount of sharing, copying, and rewriting that typify the phenomenon of *brit habat,* I fear that someone somewhere will find their words uncredited or miscredited. For this I apologize.

I would like to acknowledge the work of the Jewish Women's Resource Center, a project of the National Council of Jewish Women, New York Section, for their library, which is a national resource. Their pamphlet "Birth Ceremonies" contains many examples of *brit habat* and was an important source for me. To find out about ordering this and other publications, write to the JWRC at the NCJW, 9 East 69th Street, New York NY 10021.

Another valuable resource available from the JWRC is "Blessing the Birth of a Daughter: Jewish Naming Ceremonies for Girls," edited by Toby Fishbein Reifman, which is cited below.

Thanks to all the parents and rabbis who took the time to share ceremonies with me. Among them: Fern Amper and Eli Schaap, Aliza Arzt, Rabbi Albert Axelrad, Naomi Bar-Yam, Judith Baskin, Randee Rosenberg Freidman, Carol and Michael Katzman, Stanley H. Hellman, Rabbi Jeffrey A. Perry-Marx, Judith May, Rabbi Sandy Sasso, Rabbi Daniel Siegel and Hannah Siegel, Rabbi Paul Swerdlow, Rabbi Edward Treister and Rochelle Treister.

27. "Raba, son of Rabbi Hana, said to Abaye, 'Go forth and see how the public are accustomed to act.' " Seder Zeraim, Berakoth 45b.

28. *The Jewish Catalogs* (Volumes 1–3) published by the Jewish Publication Society of America from 1973 to 1980.

29. For an interesting discussion of ritual impurity, see Rachel Adler's article "Tumah and Taharah: Ends and Beginnings" in Elizabeth Koltun's book, *The Jewish Woman.* New York: Schocken, 1976, p. 63. One revisionist reading attributes the longer period of ritual impurity for the mothers of daughters to the fact that giving birth to a birth-giver represents a more powerful encounter with the source of life, which requires a longer separation from the mundane.

30. Rabbi Lawrence Kushner, *The River of Light, Spirituality, Judaism and the Evolution of Consciousness.* San Francisco: Harper & Row, 1980, p. xii.

31. Jewish Women's Resource Center, "Birth Ceremonies, *Brit Banot:* Covenant of Our Daughters." New York, 1985, p. 2.

32. Blu Greenberg, *How to Run a Traditional Jewish Household.* New York: Simon & Schuster, 1983, p. 248.

33. Dobrinski, pp. 3–25.

34. Toby Fishbein Reifman with Ezrat Nashim, *Blessing the Birth of a Daughter: Jewish Naming Ceremonies for Girls.* Englewood, NJ: Ezrat Nashim, 1978. Quoting an unpublished paper by Rabbi Marc Angel of the Spanish and Portuguese Synagogue in New York, p. 27.

35. Reifman, pp. 26–27. Adapted from the ceremony that appears in the *Daily and Sabbath Prayer Book* edited by Dr. David de Sola Pool. New York: Union of Sephardic Congregations. *Birkat hagomel* is recited before the ceremony.

36. Shir HaShirim Rabbah 1, 24.
37. Sasso, *op. cit.* This is one of the earliest convenantal blessings, first used in the early 1970s, written by Rabbi Sandy E. Sasso and Rabbi Dennis Sasso.
38. Mary Gendler proposed hymenectomy, piercing a girl's hymen, in an article in *Response* Magazine (Winter 1974–75). The idea was taken up by E. M. Broner in her novel *A Weave of Women* (Bantam, 1980). Another proposal for ritual ear piercing met with similar negative response; in addition to the general reluctance to cause any pain or draw any blood, pierced ears are a symbol of slavery in the Torah.
39. *Brit rehitzah* was written by Rabbis Rebecca Trachtenberg Alpert, Nancy Fuchs-Kreimer, Linda Holtzman, Sandy Levine, Joy Levitt, Debbie Prinz, Ruth Sohn, Marjorie Yudkin and Debbie Zecher. The ceremony was first published in *Menorah* magazine, 1983. A long excerpt from the ceremony appears in Susan Weidman Schneider, *Jewish and Female*. New York: Simon & Schuster, 1983, pp. 124–127.

Brit mikvah, a ceremony by Sharon and Michael Strassfeld, includes the total immersion of the baby in a tiny *mikvah*. It can be found in Reifman, pp. 16–22.
40. Adelman, pp. 63–65.
41. JWRC pamphlet.
42. See Marcia Falk's remarkable translation, *The Song of Songs, Love Poems from the Bible*. New York: Harcourt, Brace, Jovanovich, 1977, which is unfortunately out of print; it is worth checking the library for a copy.
43. Excerpted from a ceremony by Judith Baskin and Warren Ginsberg, written for their daughter and celebrated on October 13, 1985.
44. Excerpted from a ceremony by Hanna Tiferet Siegel and Rabbi Daniel Siegel written for their niece Adina Sara, who was named on December 27, 1987. A complete and annotated version of this ceremony is available from Rabbi Siegel c/o Tucker Foundation, Dartmouth College, Hanover NH 03755.
45. Exodus 32:1–3.
46. For Shabbat ceremonies, the Siegels suggest lighting two twenty-four-hour candles on Friday afternoon. Since a blessing would be inappropriate, the following selection is suggested:

"May her eyes be enlightened by Torah."
47. By Ron Laye, at the naming of his daughter, D'vora.
48. Adapted from the Sephardic prayer book.
49. Excerpted with permission from a ceremony by Rabbi Edward S. Treister, Houston, Texas, © 1986/5746.

50. Excerpted from a ceremony by Rabbi Jeffrey Perry-Marx, written for his daughter and celebrated on September 18, 1983. Rabbi Perry-Marx credits the following sources: *brit banot* by Janet Ross Marder; *brit bat* by Sue and Stephen Elwell, *brit rehitzah* (*op. cit.*), and *Gates of the Home,* a publication of the Central Conference of American Rabbis. The grandparents' prayer was written by Rabbi Sandy Sasso *(op. cit.)*.
51. From a much-quoted passage by Martin Buber.

Hiddur Mitzvah: Beautiful Touches

52. Krohn, p. 96.
53. Krohn, p. 96.
54. Rabbi Fred V. Davidow, "Blessing of a New-Born Child," Temple Beth Israel, Plattsburgh, New York.
55. For ideas and patterns, consult books on Jewish needlepoint. Patterns for other ceremonial objects can be adapted for use on a *wimpel.*

Toni Bader of Indianapolis, Indiana, designed and made a 14′ by 12″ *wimpel* to honor the birth of her son, Joshua Phillip Bader, who was born in 1979. The *wimpel* was presented—with the whole family participating—to her synagogue, Beth El Zedeck in Indianapolis, to mark Joshua's first birthday. The *wimpel* was used during the service for her oldest daughter's *bat mitzvah* in November 1986, when the family again unrolled it to its full length and explained its meaning and history.
56. Sharon Strassfeld and Michael Strassfeld, *The Second Jewish Catalog*. Philadelphia: The Jewish Publication Society of America, 1976, p. 42. Here you will also find a prayer that can be used when parents bring a *wimpel* to their synagogue.
57. Many thanks to Cantor Robert Scherr, of Temple Israel in Natick, Massachusetts, for his invaluable assistance.
58. See Marcia Falk, *The Song of Songs, Love Poems from the Bible*. New York: Harcourt Brace Jovanovich, 1977.
59. For a lovely, original interpretation of the first psalm see David Rosenberg's *Blues of the Sky*. New York: Harper & Row, 1976.
60. Reprinted with the permission of the author.
61. Reprinted with the permission of the author.
62. Reprinted with the permission of the author.
63. Reprinted with the permission of the author who grants permission for the reprinting of this poem if the copyright is printed and if notification is sent to her c/o Havurat Shalom, 113 College Avenue, Somerville MA 02144.
64. Reprinted with the permission of the author.
65. Reprinted with the permission of the author.
66. Reprinted by permission of the author.

PART FOUR: SIMCHA: JOY

Simcha Means Party

1. Krohn, p. 5.
2. Dobrinski, p. 6.
3. A full version of the special *birkat hamazon* that follows a *bris* is given in Krohn, pp. 141–160. Also see Strassfeld and Strassfeld, *The Second Jewish Catalog,* p. 28.
4. Thanks to Rochelle Treister, proprietor of Elijah's Cup, a Judaica gallery in Houston, Texas, for her suggestions, which include the silver and brass dreydels. There is a small but growing number of Judaica shops, like Elijah's Cup and Kolbo in Brookline, Massachusetts, that sell wonderful hand-crafted gifts made by American and Israeli artists. Most synagogue gift shops and Jewish bookstores carry books, games and tapes for children.

Celebrations and Customs

5. Many thanks to Carol and Michael Katzman of Omaha, Nebraska, whose letter introduced this idea to me. The Katzmans have "twinned" birth ceremonies for each of their three children. Of their most recent experience, in 1985, they write, "We were matched up to Rita and Boris Deviatov, whose daughter Sarah was born six weeks before our Rachel. We have been corresponding with the Deviatovs for the last year and a half. My biggest fear is that eleven and a half years from now, we will be twinning Rachel's *bat mitvah* with Sarah Daviatov's."
6. Thirty days was the biblical measure of a child's viability. Babies younger than a month old were very vulnerable to death, and it was considered inappropriate to dedicate to God something or someone so at risk.
7. In the past, one searched out a *kohane* in need of the money exchanged during the ceremony, thus fulfilling two *mitzvot* at once; charity and redemption (Gottlieb, p. 59). If, on the other hand, the parents were poor, the *kohane* might return the money after the ceremony. (This could not be a condition of the exchange, however, or else the ceremony would be invalid.) In the Middle Ages, rabbinic authorities decreed that the money must be returned to the father, since it was no longer possible for any *kohane* to prove his descent. (Schauss, p. 59)
8. Often the rabbi or *kohane* begins the ritual with a short address or with a few lines of responsive reading. For an example, see Gottlieb, p. 55. For other sources, consult your rabbi and/or look at various rabbis' manuals.
9. Rabbi Marc S. Golub and Rabbi Norman Cohen, "Kiddush Petter Rechem: An Alternative to Pidyon Haben," *CCAR Journal,* Winter, 1973,

p. 72. The article contains a ceremony of the same name, written by the authors.
10. Sasso, *Call Them Builders,* pp. 23–24.
11. Sasso, *op. cit.* Also see the ceremony by Daniel I. Leifer and Myra Leifer, published in Koltun, pp. 26–29.
12. Krohn, p. 73.
13. Krohn, p. 95.
14. Schauss, p. 46.
15. Leo Trepp, *The Complete Book of Jewish Observance.* New York: Behrman House Inc./Summit Books, 1980, p. 226.
16. Adelman, pp. 50–55.
17. Magical talismans and customs like *Vach Nacht* were undertaken to protect a baby and its family against Lilith, Adam's first wife who hunts all babies in revenge for the deaths of her own demon children, who are killed daily. For vivid details about Lilith and the dangers of childbed, see Schauss, pp. 67–74.

Announcements

Thanks to Elaine Adler, Jonathan Kremer, Betsy Platkin Teutsch and all the calligraphers who generously shared their work and ideas with me. A list of calligraphers is found at the end of this book. Thanks also to the parents whose announcements are quoted, excerpted, and featured.
18. Betsy Platkin Teutsch.
19. This poem has been reproduced, without attribution, and with some variations, all over the country.

PART FIVE: MODERN LIFE

Special thanks to Rabbi Daniel Shevitz for his insight, as well as for his thoughtful comments on an early draft of this chapter. Thanks also to Phyllis Nissen and Rabbi Susan Abramson of the Stars of David; Phyllis Lowenstein, executive director of International Adoptions, Inc., in Waltham MA; and Alma Orchnick of the Jewish Family and Children's Service in Boston.

A book that addresses many of the issues raised in this section from a traditional perspective is, *And Hannah Wept: Infertility, Adoption and the Jewish Couple* by Rabbi Michael Gold: Philadelphia: Jewish Publication Society of America, 1988.

Adoption

1. Rabbi Daniel Shevitz, "A Guide for the Jewish Adoptive Parent," *Response,* No. 48, Spring, 1985, pp. 107–126. This is an excellent source

for *halachic* information as well as a sensitively written account by an adoptive parent.

2. *Tshuvot haRashba hameyuchasot laRamban* #38, from Shevitz, above.

3. For specific information regarding the adoption of Jewish children, see Shevitz, op cit. Also, consult your rabbi.

4. Rabbi Aryeh Kaplan, *Waters of Eden: The Mystery of the Mikvah.* New York: National Conference of Synagogue Youth/Union of Orthodox Jewish Congregations, 1976, p. 35.

5. Gottlieb, p. 74.

6. Janelle Bohrod, "Janelle Bohrod's Story," *Startracks,* Spring, 1986, pp. 5–7.

7. Shevitz, p. 114.

8. Patricia Schaffer, *Chag Sameach!* Berkeley: Tabor Sarah Books, 1985. To order, send $4.95 for the book plus $1.25 for shipping (.50 for shipping additional copies) to Tabor Sarah Books, 2419 Jefferson Avenue, Berkeley CA 94703.

9. Thanks to Rabbi Daniel Shevitz and Susan Shevitz, who wrote the ceremony upon which this one is based.

PART SIX: THE FIRST YEAR

The First Year

Thanks to the Jewish Women's Resource Center of the National Council of Jewish Women, New York Section; and especially to Naomi Bar-Yam, Fern Amper and Eli Schaap, and Marga Kamm, whose ceremonies, *divrei* Torah, and comments inform much of this chapter.

1. A traditional prayer, based on various biblical quotations and associated with the giving of the *wimpel* may be found in the *Second Jewish Catalog,* Sharon Strassfeld, Michael Strassfeld. Philadelphia: Jewish Publication Society of America, 1976, p. 42.

2. Pesikta de Rav Kahana 12:2.

3. Thanks to Fern Amper and Eli Schaap, for permission to quote from the ceremony for their daughter, Yona, which was held on December 11, 1983.

INDEX